RECIPES & REMEDIES

PRESCRIPTIONS FOR HEALTHY LIVING

RECIPES & REMEDIES

PRESCRIPTIONS FOR HEALTHY LIVING

A COLLECTION OF RECIPES PRESENTED BY
THE CALIFORNIA PHARMACISTS ASSOCIATION

Recipes and Remedies
Prescriptions for Healthy Living

Copyright © 2000
California Pharmacists Association
1112 I Street, Suite 300, Sacramento, California 95814
www.cpha.com
(916) 444-7811

California Pharmacists Association Staff:
Elizabeth Johnson, Pharm.D.
Jennifer Klein Walker

Cookbook Committee:
Anna Charuk Kowblansky, R.Ph., MS
Ruth M. Conroy, Pharm.D.
Debby Johnson, Pharmacist
Robert Nickell, Pharmacist
Ralph Saroyan, Pharmacist Educator

Healthy Tips Consultant: Giselle Haettig, Pharm.D.

Food Photographer: Brooks Photo
Food Photography Assistant: Josh Taylor
Food and Prop Stylist: Mandy Sabbadini

Pharmacy Memorabilia Courtesy of the
Donald F. Salvatori California Pharmacy Museum

Library of Congress Number: 00-131775
ISBN: 0-9700268-0-3

Designed, Edited, and Manufactured by Favorite Recipes® Press
an imprint of

FRP

P.O. Box 301542, Nashville, Tennessee 37230
800-358-0560

Project Manager: Debbie Van Mol
Book Design: Dave Malone, Scott Dye
Art Director: Steve Newman

Manufactured in the United States of America
First Printing: 2000   15,000 copies

TABLE OF CONTENTS

PREFACE

Recipes & Remedies: Prescriptions for Healthy Living is a one-of-a-kind cookbook that no household should be without! The intent is for this to be an all-purpose reference for cooking tips and for healthy living.

So, why did pharmacists create this cookbook?

Just as the pharmacy profession continues to evolve, so do the ways people eat and live. Pharmacists are moving beyond their traditional role of just dispensing medications into a position of being proactive health care providers. Whether they're providing a patient consultation or offering advice on disease management and prevention, pharmacists are dedicating themselves to their patients' health and well being. Maybe this is why pharmacists have been ranked as the number one most trusted professional for ten years in a row.

This cookbook, an extension of pharmacists' commitment to patient wellness, offers tips ranging from proper medication storage to common food and herb interactions. Also included are ways to lighten up recipes based on your health needs. The fact of the matter is that pharmacists play an integral part in your health care management and in your life.

We hope that you will benefit from this multifunctional cookbook and that, with the support of readers like you, this will be the first of many editions.

MISSION STATEMENT

The California Pharmacists Association is the largest state

pharmacy association in the nation and the professional

society representing all pharmacists in California.

The mission of the association is to act as the leader

in advocating the role of the pharmacist as an essential

provider of health care and to support pharmacists

in providing optimal pharmaceutical care.

APRICOT PICKUPS

8 ounces cream cheese, softened
$^1/_4$ cup fruit chutney
2 tablespoons chopped green onions
1 (6-ounce) package dried apricots
$^1/_2$ cup water
$^1/_2$ cup finely chopped pecans

Beat the cream cheese in a mixing bowl until smooth. Stir in the chutney and green onions. Chill, covered, for 1 hour. Combine the apricots and water in a saucepan. Bring to a boil, stirring occasionally; reduce heat.

Simmer, covered, for 4 minutes or until the apricots are plump; drain. Pat dry with paper towels. Let stand until cool. Spoon the cream cheese mixture into the apricots. Top with the pecans. Arrange on a serving platter. Chill, covered, until firm.

YIELD: 40 SERVINGS

BLEU CHEESE WALNUT GRAPES

4 ounces bleu cheese, crumbled
3 ounces cream cheese, softened
24 large seedless green grapes
1 cup chopped walnuts, toasted

Beat the bleu cheese and cream cheese in a mixing bowl until blended. Chill, covered, for 1 hour. Shape approximately 1 tablespoon of the cheese mixture around each grape. Roll in the walnuts. Arrange the grapes on a serving platter. Chill, covered, for 1 hour.

YIELD: 24 SERVINGS

CHERRY TOMATOES WITH HERBED CREAM CHEESE

8 ounces cream cheese, softened
1 tablespoon lemon juice
1 scallion, chopped
2 garlic cloves, minced
1 cup minced fresh herbs
2 pints cherry tomatoes

Combine the cream cheese, lemon juice, scallion, garlic and herbs in a food processor container. Process until smooth. Spoon the cream cheese mixture into a pastry bag fitted with a star tip.

Remove the tomato stems. Cut an X in the opposite ends of the tomatoes and squeeze out the seeds. Pipe the filling into the tomatoes. Arrange on a serving platter. Chill, covered, until serving time.

YIELD: 12 SERVINGS

LIGHTEN UP

Substitute nonfat cream cheese for the cream cheese and increase the minced fresh herbs to 1 1/2 cups to enhance the flavor.

ENDIVE ANTIPASTO

2 heads Belgian endive, separated into spears
1 (6-ounce) can marinated artichokes, drained, chopped
1/2 cup chopped zucchini
1/3 cup chopped salami
1/4 cup chopped black olives
3 tablespoons creamy Italian salad dressing

Rinse the endive, pat dry with paper towels and place in a sealable plastic bag. Chill in the refrigerator. Combine the artichokes, zucchini, salami, olives and salad dressing in a bowl and mix well.

Spoon the artichoke mixture onto the stem end of each endive spear. Arrange in a spoke fashion on a serving platter.

YIELD: 32 SERVINGS

2$^1/_2$ pounds large shrimp, steamed, peeled, deveined
1 onion, thinly sliced
1$^1/_4$ cups vegetable oil
$^3/_4$ cup rice wine vinegar
2$^1/_2$ tablespoons undrained capers
2$^1/_2$ teaspoons celery seeds
1$^1/_2$ teaspoons salt
8 bay leaves
Tabasco sauce to taste
6 to 8 lettuce leaves

Mix the shrimp and onion in a bowl. Combine the oil, rice wine vinegar, capers, celery seeds, salt, bay leaves and Tabasco sauce in a bowl and mix well. Pour over the shrimp mixture and toss to coat. Marinate, covered, in the refrigerator for 24 hours, stirring occasionally.

Drain the shrimp and discard the marinade. Arrange the shrimp on a lettuce-lined serving platter. Serve immediately. You may add fresh whole mushrooms and/or artichoke hearts for variety.

YIELD: 10 SERVINGS

Green Olive Salsa

1 (20-ounce) can green salad olives, drained
6 to 8 large tomatoes, peeled, finely chopped
2 (4-ounce) cans diced green chiles, drained
2 bunches green onions, finely chopped
3 tablespoons olive oil
2 to 3 teaspoons garlic salt
2 teaspoons lemon pepper
1 to 1$^1/_2$ cups red wine vinegar

Process the olives in a food processor until finely chopped. Combine the olives, tomatoes, chiles, green onions, olive oil, garlic salt and lemon pepper in a bowl and mix well. Add just enough of the wine vinegar to cover the ingredients.

Chill, covered, until serving time. Serve with Pita Crisps (below). You may store the salsa for up to 1 month in the refrigerator.

YIELD: 20 SERVINGS

Pita Crisps

5 (5-inch) pita rounds, split
1 tablespoon basil
1 tablespoon oregano
1 teaspoon garlic powder
1 teaspoon dillweed

Spray both sides of the pita rounds with butter-flavored nonstick cooking spray. Cut each round into 6 wedges. Combine the basil, oregano, garlic powder and dillweed in a bowl and mix well. Add the pita wedges and toss to coat.

Arrange the pita wedges in a single layer on a nonstick baking sheet. Bake at 350 degrees for 5 to 8 minutes or until crisp.

YIELD: 60 CRISPS

Margarita Guacamole

2 ripe avocados
3 tablespoons lime juice
1 tablespoon tequila
2 fresh jalapeño chiles, seeded, minced
6 green onions, finely chopped
1 tablespoon minced fresh cilantro
1 garlic clove, minced
$1/4$ teaspoon salt

Mash the avocados in a bowl. Stir in the lime juice. Add the tequila, chiles, green onions, cilantro, garlic and salt and mix well. Chill, covered, until serving time. Serve with corn chips or tortilla chips.

Yield: 8 ($1/4$-cup) servings

Tres Cheese Ball

Lighten Up

Use nonfat cream cheese for the cream cheese. Decrease the walnuts to $1/3$ cup but toast them to intensify the flavor.

8 ounces cream cheese, softened
4 ounces bleu cheese, crumbled
4 ounces sharp Cheddar cheese, shredded
$2/3$ cup chopped walnuts
$1 1/2$ teaspoons Worcestershire sauce
$1 1/2$ teaspoons minced onion
Minced fresh parsley

Combine the cream cheese, bleu cheese, Cheddar cheese, $1/3$ cup of the walnuts, Worcestershire sauce and onion in a food processor container. Process until mixed. Shape the cheese mixture into a ball. Roll in the remaining $1/3$ cup walnuts and parsley.

Chill, wrapped in plastic wrap, until firm. Let stand at room temperature for 15 to 30 minutes before serving. Serve with assorted party crackers.

Yield: 16 servings

Chili Chicken Torta

2 teaspoons chicken bouillon granules
$^1/_2$ cup hot water
24 ounces cream cheese, softened
$1^1/_2$ teaspoons chili powder
$^1/_2$ teaspoon Tabasco sauce
2 eggs
1 cup finely chopped cooked chicken
1 (4-ounce) can diced green chiles, drained
$^1/_2$ to $^3/_4$ cup salsa
$^1/_2$ to $^3/_4$ cup shredded Cheddar cheese
3 green onions, finely chopped

Dissolve the bouillon granules in the hot water. Beat the cream cheese, chili powder and Tabasco sauce in a bowl until creamy. Add the eggs and beat until blended. Beat in the bouillon. Stir in the chicken and chiles.

Spoon the chicken mixture into a 9-inch springform pan sprayed with nonstick cooking spray. Bake at 325 degrees for 30 minutes or until set. Let stand for 15 minutes. Run a sharp knife around the edge of the pan. Remove the side. Place the torta on a serving platter.

Spread the salsa over the top of the torta. Sprinkle with the Cheddar cheese and green onions. Serve warm or chilled with assorted party crackers.

YIELD: 16 SERVINGS

Lighten Up

Substitute reduced-fat cream cheese for the cream cheese and 4 egg whites for the eggs. Decrease the Cheddar cheese to $^1/_3$ cup, using sharp Cheddar cheese for more flavor.

EGGPLANT CAVIAR

1¹/₄ pounds eggplant
1 large tomato, chopped
3 green onions, finely chopped
¹/₂ stalk celery, finely chopped
¹/₃ cup finely chopped green bell pepper
1 garlic clove, minced
2 teaspoons vegetable oil
1 teaspoon lemon juice
¹/₂ teaspoon salt
¹/₂ teaspoon freshly ground pepper

Prick the eggplant on all sides with a fork. Arrange on a baking sheet. Bake at 400 degrees for 45 minutes or until tender, turning several times. Let stand until cool. Peel the eggplant and finely chop.

Combine the eggplant, tomato, green onions, celery, bell pepper and garlic in a bowl and mix gently. Stir in the oil, lemon juice, salt and pepper. Chill, covered, for 1 hour or until serving time. Serve with assorted party crackers and/or crudités.

YIELD: 12 (¹/₄-CUP) SERVINGS

Sun-Dried Tomato and Basil Spread

12 ounces feta cheese, crumbled
8 ounces cream cheese, softened
1 cup (2 sticks) butter or margarine
3 tablespoons dry vermouth
2 garlic cloves, finely chopped
1 shallot, finely chopped
Freshly ground pepper to taste
Tabasco sauce to taste
1 (8-ounce) jar oil-packed sun-dried tomatoes, drained, minced
1 cup prepared or homemade pesto
1/2 cup sunflower kernels, toasted

Beat the feta cheese, cream cheese, butter, vermouth, garlic and shallot in a mixing bowl until mixed, scraping the bowl occasionally. Season with pepper and Tabasco sauce. Stir in the sun-dried tomatoes, pesto and sunflower kernels.

Spoon the sun-dried tomato mixture into an oiled 4- or 5-cup mold. Chill, covered, until firm. Invert onto a lettuce-lined serving platter. Serve with assorted party crackers and/or crusty French bread.

YIELD: 25 SERVINGS

LIGHTEN UP

Replace oil-packed sun-dried tomatoes with rehydrated sun-dried tomatoes, butter with margarine and cream cheese with reduced-fat cream cheese to decrease fat and cholesterol.

ARTICHOKE-FILLED APPETIZER LOAF

1 long loaf French bread
1/3 cup butter or margarine
2 teaspoons sesame seeds
1/2 teaspoon garlic powder
1 (14-ounce) can artichoke hearts, drained, chopped
4 ounces Monterey Jack cheese, shredded
3/4 cup freshly grated Parmesan cheese
1/2 cup sour cream
2 ounces sharp Cheddar cheese, shredded

Slice the bread loaf lengthwise into halves. Remove the centers carefully, leaving two 1-inch shells. Arrange the shells on a baking sheet. Crumble the bread from the centers.

Heat the butter in a skillet until melted. Stir in the sesame seeds and garlic powder. Cook until the sesame seeds are light brown, stirring constantly. Stir in the artichokes, Monterey Jack cheese, Parmesan cheese and sour cream. Add the crumbled bread and mix well.

Spoon the artichoke mixture into the bread shells. Bake, covered with foil, at 350 degrees for 25 minutes; remove cover. Sprinkle with the Cheddar cheese. Bake just until the cheese melts. Cut each half into 12 slices. Serve immediately.

YIELD: 24 SLICES

Artichoke Squares

2 (6-ounce) jars marinated artichoke hearts
4 eggs, beaten
1 cup cottage cheese
1 small onion, finely chopped
1/8 teaspoon marjoram
1/8 teaspoon basil
1/8 teaspoon thyme
1/8 teaspoon rosemary

Drain the artichokes, reserving 2 tablespoons of the marinade. Chop the artichokes. Combine the artichokes, reserved marinade, eggs, cottage cheese, onion, marjoram, basil, thyme and rosemary in a bowl and mix well.

Spoon the artichoke mixture into a greased 8x8-inch baking dish. Bake at 350 degrees for 30 minutes or until set and light brown. Cut into 1-inch squares. Serve hot or at room temperature.

YIELD: 64 SQUARES

THAI CHICKEN AND SHRIMP SKEWERS WITH PEANUT SAUCE

CHICKEN AND SHRIMP

$1^1/2$ pounds boneless skinless chicken breasts
1 cup teriyaki sauce
$3^1/2$ tablespoons fresh lime juice
4 garlic cloves, minced
2 tablespoons minced gingerroot
2 tablespoons light brown sugar
24 medium shrimp, peeled, deveined

PEANUT SAUCE

1 (16-ounce) can chicken broth
1 cup creamy peanut butter
$1/4$ cup fresh lime juice
3 tablespoons light brown sugar
2 tablespoons plus 1 teaspoon soy sauce
2 tablespoons chopped gingerroot
$1/2$ teaspoon red pepper flakes

To prepare the chicken and shrimp, cut the chicken into $1/2$-inch strips. Combine the teriyaki sauce, lime juice, garlic, gingerroot and brown sugar in a bowl and mix well. Add the chicken and shrimp and toss to coat.

Marinate, covered, in the refrigerator for 30 to 60 minutes, stirring occasionally; drain. Thread the chicken and shrimp separately on 36 skewers. Grill over hot coals for 3 minutes per side or until the chicken is cooked through and the shrimp turn pink. Arrange the skewers on a lettuce-lined serving platter.

To prepare the sauce, combine the broth, peanut butter, lime juice, brown sugar, soy sauce, gingerroot and red pepper in a saucepan and mix well. Cook over medium heat for 5 to 6 minutes or until heated through, stirring frequently. Spoon into a small bowl and place in the center of the serving platter.

YIELD: 12 SERVINGS

CRAB IMPERIAL MUSHROOMS

45 large mushrooms
$3/4$ cup mayonnaise
1 egg, beaten
$1^1/_2$ tablespoons chopped fresh parsley
$1^1/_2$ teaspoons lemon juice
1 teaspoon dry mustard
$1/_4$ teaspoon baking powder
$1/_4$ teaspoon Worcestershire sauce
$1/_8$ teaspoon cayenne pepper
1 pound lump crab meat
1 cup fresh bread crumbs

Remove the stems from the mushrooms. Arrange the mushroom caps in 2 greased 9x13-inch baking pans.

Combine the mayonnaise, egg, parsley, lemon juice, dry mustard, baking powder, Worcestershire sauce and cayenne pepper in a bowl and mix well. Add the crab meat and mix gently. Fill each mushroom cap with approximately 1 tablespoon of the crab meat mixture. Sprinkle with the bread crumbs.

Bake at 350 degrees for 15 to 18 minutes or until light brown. Arrange on a serving platter. Serve immediately.

YIELD: 45 MUSHROOMS

Rx FACTS ABOUT HERBAL PRODUCTS

Examples of prescription drug interactions with herbal products:

❋ Cat's Claw (often used for viral infections) can greatly decrease blood pressure when taken with high blood pressure medication, and may cause dizziness and fainting.

❋ Gotu Kola (often used for wound healing) can cause a dangerous decrease in blood sugar when taken with anti-diabetic medications.

FETA CHEESE PILLOWS

16 ounces cream cheese, softened
8 ounces feta cheese, crumbled
1 egg
$1^1/4$ cups ($2^1/2$ sticks) plus 3 tablespoons butter or margarine, melted
1 (16-ounce) package frozen phyllo pastry, thawed

Combine the cream cheese, feta cheese, egg and 3 tablespoons of the butter in a mixing bowl. Beat at medium speed until smooth, scraping the bowl occasionally.

Unroll the phyllo and cover with waxed paper topped with a damp tea towel to prevent it from drying out, removing 2 sheets at a time. Brush each sheet with melted butter. Cut each sheet into 2-inch-wide strips. Place 1 teaspoon of the cream cheese mixture at the end of each strip. Fold the corner over to form a triangle and continue to fold in triangles to the end of the strip. Arrange on an ungreased baking sheet. Bake at 350 degrees for 20 minutes or until golden brown.

You may bake in advance and store, covered, in the freezer or refrigerator for future use. Reheat at 350 degrees for 10 minutes. Add chopped cooked spinach to the filling for variety.

YIELD: 6 DOZEN PILLOWS

PARMESAN WALNUT BRUSCHETTA

$3/4$ cup freshly grated Parmesan cheese
$3/4$ cup olive oil
$1/2$ cup finely chopped walnuts
16 ($1/2$-inch) slices French bread

Combine $1/2$ cup of the cheese, $1/4$ cup of the olive oil and $1/4$ cup of the walnuts in a food processor container. Process until almost smooth.

Brush both sides of the bread slices with the remaining $1/2$ cup olive oil. Arrange on a baking sheet. Broil for 30 seconds on each side or until light brown. Spread the slices with the cheese mixture. Sprinkle with the remaining $1/4$ cup cheese and remaining $1/4$ cup walnuts. Broil for 30 seconds or until the cheese begins to melt. Serve immediately.

YIELD: 16 SERVINGS

MICHELOTTI'S NORTHERN ITALIAN-STYLE PIZZA

Carlo Michelotti, R.Ph., MPH, Chief Executive Officer of the California Pharmacists Association, donated this recipe.

1^1/$_2$ cups lukewarm water
1 teaspoon sugar
1 envelope dry yeast
4 cups King Arthur bread flour
1 tablespoon olive oil
1 teaspoon salt

Combine ^{1}/$_4$ cup of the lukewarm water and sugar in a bowl and mix well. Add the yeast, stirring until dissolved. Let stand until the volume has doubled. Stir in the remaining 1^1/$_4$ cups lukewarm water, flour, olive oil and salt. Knead for 5 minutes; the dough should be slightly tacky.

Shape the dough into a ball. Place in a greased bowl, turning to coat the surface. Let rise, covered with a damp tea towel or plastic wrap, for 2 hours or until doubled in bulk. Divide the dough into 4 equal portions. Pat each portion into a thin round and place each round on a pizza stone. The use of a pizza stone is highly recommended as a higher quality product will result than if a metal pan is used.

It is recommended to lightly sprinkle the dough with virgin olive oil and then top with traditional FRESHLY shredded mozzarella cheese. Then add no more than three of your favorite toppings, such as prosciutto, thinly-sliced Roma tomatoes, caramelized onions, artichoke hearts, mushrooms or anchovies. Drizzle lightly with additional olive oil. Bake at 500 degrees for 8 to 10 minutes or until brown and bubbly. If using a wood-fired oven, bake at 850 degrees for approximately 3 minutes.

YIELD: 4 INDIVIDUAL PIZZAS

CHICKEN AND GREEN CHILE PINWHEELS

4 boneless skinless chicken breasts
16 ounces cream cheese, softened
1¹/₂ cups shredded sharp Cheddar cheese
1 (4-ounce) can chopped black olives, drained
1 (4-ounce) can pimento-stuffed green olives, drained, chopped
¹/₂ (4-ounce) can diced green chiles
5 or 6 scallions with tops, finely chopped
10 (10-inch) flour tortillas

Poach the chicken in a small amount of water in a saucepan until tender. Drain and chop the chicken.

Beat the cream cheese and Cheddar cheese in a mixing bowl until smooth, scraping the bowl occasionally. Stir in the chicken, olives, chiles and scallions. Spread the cheese mixture to within ¹/₈ inch of the edge of each tortilla. Roll to enclose the filling. Wrap each tortilla individually in plastic wrap. Chill for 8 to 10 hours.

Cut each tortilla roll into 8 slices just before serving. Arrange the pinwheels on a serving platter. Serve with salsa, sour cream and/or guacamole. You may prepare up to 3 days in advance and store in the refrigerator. Slice just before serving.

YIELD: 80 PINWHEELS

SOUTHWESTERN SPINACH ROLLERS

2 (10-ounce) packages frozen chopped spinach, thawed, drained
8 ounces cream cheese, softened
1 cup sour cream
1 cup mayonnaise
1 (8-ounce) can chopped water chestnuts, drained
1 (4-ounce) can diced green chiles, drained
1/2 cup chopped black olives
1 envelope ranch salad dressing mix
4 green onions with tops, chopped
2 teaspoons chili powder
1 teaspoon minced garlic
1 teaspoon minced jalapeño chile
1/4 teaspoon Tabasco sauce
10 (10-inch) flour tortillas

Press the excess moisture from the spinach. Beat the cream cheese, sour cream and mayonnaise in a mixing bowl until smooth. Stir in the spinach, water chestnuts, green chiles, olives, salad dressing mix, green onions, chili powder, garlic, jalapeño chile and Tabasco sauce.

Spread the spinach mixture to within $1/8$ inch of the edge of each tortilla. Roll to enclose the filling. Wrap each tortilla individually in plastic wrap. Chill, covered, for 8 to 10 hours. Cut each tortilla roll into 8 slices. Arrange on a serving platter.

YIELD: 80 ROLLERS

LIGHTEN UP

Substitute reduced-fat cream cheese for the cream cheese, plain nonfat yogurt for the sour cream and reduced-fat mayonnaise for the mayonnaise.

CHICKEN AND LEEK SOUP

1 pound boneless skinless chicken breasts, chopped
3 medium leeks, chopped
3 garlic cloves, finely chopped
4 cups thickly sliced mushrooms
3 cups reduced-sodium chicken broth
$1/3$ cup dry white wine
$2^1/2$ cups skim milk
$1/2$ cup flour
2 tablespoons dry sherry
$1/4$ teaspoon salt
$1/4$ teaspoon white pepper

Spray a saucepan with nonstick cooking spray. Heat over high heat until hot. Add the chicken, leeks and garlic. Sauté for 10 minutes. Add the mushrooms and mix well. Sauté for 5 minutes longer. Stir in the broth and white wine. Bring to a boil; reduce heat. Simmer for 10 minutes, stirring occasionally.

Add the skim milk to the flour in a bowl, whisking constantly until blended. Stir into the chicken mixture. Cook over medium heat for 10 minutes or until thickened, stirring constantly. Add the sherry, salt and white pepper and mix well. Ladle into soup bowls. Serve with crackers.

YIELD: 6 SERVINGS

MUSHROOM AND WILD RICE SOUP

1 onion, chopped
1/4 cup olive oil
16 ounces mushrooms, sliced
1/2 cup thinly sliced celery
6 cups chicken broth
1/2 cup cooked wild rice
1/2 teaspoon salt
1/2 teaspoon curry powder
1/2 teaspoon dry mustard
1/2 cup flour
2 cups skim milk
3 tablespoons sherry

Sauté the onion in the olive oil in a large saucepan until tender. Stir in the mushrooms and celery. Sauté for 2 minutes longer. Add 5 cups of the broth, wild rice, salt, curry powder and dry mustard and mix well.

Simmer for 5 minutes, stirring occasionally. Whisk the flour into the remaining 1 cup broth in a bowl until blended. Add to the mushroom mixture and mix well. Simmer for 10 minutes or until thickened, stirring occasionally. Stir in the skim milk and sherry. Simmer just until heated through, stirring constantly. Ladle into soup bowls. Serve with crusty French bread.

YIELD: 6 SERVINGS

LIGHTEN UP

Decrease the fat grams and sodium by omitting 2 tablespoons olive oil and sautéing the onion in a nonstick skillet sprayed with nonstick olive oil cooking spray. Substitute nonfat reduced-sodium chicken broth for the chicken broth.

Vidalia Onion and Wild Mushroom Soup

6 cups reduced-sodium chicken broth
1/4 cup mixed dried wild mushrooms
2 cups sliced Vidalia onions
1/3 cup finely minced fresh sage
1 teaspoon olive oil
1 cup dry white wine
2 tablespoons minced fresh Italian parsley
1/8 teaspoon freshly ground pepper

Heat 1 cup of the broth in a saucepan until hot. Pour over the wild mushrooms in a heatproof bowl. Let stand for 30 minutes. Drain, reserving the liquid. Chop the mushrooms finely.

Cook the onions and sage in the olive oil in a skillet over low heat for 20 minutes or until the onions are tender, stirring frequently. Stir in the remaining 5 cups broth, reserved liquid, white wine, parsley and pepper. Simmer, covered, for 40 minutes, stirring occasionally. Ladle into soup bowls. Serve with crackers.

YIELD: 4 SERVINGS

Seafood Gazpacho

4 cups tomato juice
1 1/4 cups chopped tomatoes
1/4 cup chopped yellow bell pepper
1/4 cup chopped red bell pepper
1/4 cup chopped green bell pepper
1/4 cup chopped peeled cucumber
1/4 cup chopped red onion
1/4 cup lime juice
1 tablespoon chopped jalapeño chile
1 cup fresh bread crumbs
3 tablespoons olive oil
1 teaspoon minced garlic
3/4 teaspoon cumin
Salt and pepper to taste
4 ounces cooked scallops
4 ounces deveined peeled cooked shrimp
4 ounces cooked crab meat
1 small avocado, chopped

Combine the tomato juice, tomatoes, bell peppers, cucumber, onion, lime juice and chile in a bowl and mix well. Stir in the bread crumbs, olive oil, garlic, cumin, salt and pepper. Chill, covered, for 8 to 10 hours.

Stir the scallops, shrimp and crab meat into the gazpacho. Ladle into chilled soup bowls. Top with the avocado. Serve with crusty French bread.

Yield: 8 servings

Rx Facts About Cancer Screening

✳ *Breast Cancer: A yearly breast exam by a health practitioner is recommended for women over forty. Mammography is recommended every one to two years for women fifty to seventy-five. A mammogram can detect a lump in a woman's breast up to two years before a woman can feel it herself.*

✳ *Cervical Cancer: All women should have a yearly Pap smear starting at age eighteen or when they begin having sex. Pap testing can detect precancerous changes in the cervix early enough for successful treatment.*

GARDEN TOMATO AND ZUCCHINI SOUP

$^1/_2$ cup sliced celery
3 shallots, chopped
2 large garlic cloves, minced
1 tablespoon butter or margarine
4 cups reduced-sodium chicken stock
3 tomatoes, chopped
1 unpeeled zucchini, thinly sliced
1 tablespoon tomato paste
1 teaspoon chopped fresh Italian parsley
1 teaspoon chopped fresh cilantro
1 bay leaf
6 tablespoons reduced-fat plain yogurt

Sauté the celery, shallots and garlic in the butter in a large saucepan until the celery and shallots are tender. Stir in the stock, tomatoes, zucchini, tomato paste, parsley, cilantro and bay leaf.

Simmer for 2 hours, stirring occasionally. Discard the bay leaf. Ladle into soup bowls. Top each serving with 1 tablespoon of the yogurt. Serve with crackers.

YIELD: 6 SERVINGS

TURKEY TORTILLA SOUP

1 cup chopped onion
1 teaspoon vegetable oil
1 (4-ounce) can diced green chiles, drained
1 envelope taco seasoning mix
1 (16-ounce) can diced tomatoes
6 cups turkey broth
1 (10-ounce) package frozen whole kernel corn
2 cups chopped cooked turkey
1/2 cup chopped fresh cilantro
8 ounces unsalted tortilla chips, broken
1 cup shredded Monterey Jack cheese

Sauté the onion in the oil in a large saucepan for 3 to 4 minutes or until tender. Stir in the chiles and seasoning mix. Cook for 1 minute, stirring occasionally. Add the undrained tomatoes and broth. Bring to a boil; reduce heat to low. Stir in the corn and turkey.

Simmer for 5 minutes, stirring occasionally. Add the cilantro and mix well. Ladle into soup bowls. Top with the tortilla chips and sprinkle with the cheese.

To make Chicken Tortilla Soup, substitute chicken broth for the turkey broth and 2 cups chopped cooked chicken for the turkey.

YIELD: 8 SERVINGS

LIGHTEN UP

Substitute reduced-sodium nonfat turkey broth for the turkey broth, nonfat shredded mozzarella cheese for the Monterey Jack cheese and no-added-salt tomatoes for the diced tomatoes. Omit the commercially prepared tortilla chips and make your own. Cut 8 corn tortillas into strips and spray with nonstick cooking spray. Bake until crisp or use baked tortilla chips.

Mexicali Black Bean Chili

Lighten Up

Omit the oil and sauté reduced-fat turkey kielbasa and the vegetables in a nonstick skillet sprayed with nonstick cooking spray. Substitute ground turkey for the ground pork. Decrease the sodium by substituting 1 pound cooked dried black beans for the canned black beans and using no-added-salt diced tomatoes.

2 tablespoons vegetable oil
1 pound chorizo or kielbasa, cut into $1/2$-inch slices
$1^1/2$ pounds lean ground beef
$1^1/2$ pounds ground pork
3 onions, chopped
2 large green bell peppers, chopped
3 garlic cloves, chopped
2 jalapeño chiles, seeded, chopped
2 (14-ounce) cans diced tomatoes
1 (12-ounce) can beer
2 tablespoons chili powder
2 teaspoons cumin
1 teaspoon salt
$1/2$ teaspoon freshly ground pepper
2 (16-ounce) cans black beans, drained, rinsed
3 cups frozen whole kernel corn
40 pimento-stuffed green olives, cut into halves

Heat 1 tablespoon of the oil in a skillet over medium heat until hot. Add the chorizo. Cook for 10 minutes or until brown, stirring frequently; drain. Remove the sausage to a platter. Brown the ground beef and ground pork in the same skillet, stirring until crumbly; drain. Remove the ground beef mixture to a colander. Rinse with boiling water; drain.

Sauté the onions, bell peppers, garlic and chiles in the remaining 1 tablespoon oil in a stockpot for 5 minutes or until the vegetables are tender. Add the chorizo, ground beef mixture, undrained tomatoes, beer, chili powder, cumin, salt and pepper and mix well.

Cook over low heat for 1 hour, stirring occasionally. Stir in the beans, corn and olives. Cook for 15 minutes longer, stirring occasionally. Ladle into chili bowls. Garnish with chopped avocado, additional chopped onion, shredded Cheddar cheese, shredded Monterey Jack cheese and/or tortilla chips. Serve with crackers or corn bread.

Yield: 12 servings

Italian Vegetable Stew

1 large red bell pepper, finely chopped
1 large green bell pepper, finely chopped
$^1/_3$ cup plus 2 teaspoons olive oil
1 cup frozen whole kernel corn, thawed
Salt and pepper to taste
2 medium onions, chopped
6 garlic cloves, chopped
1 (35-ounce) can Italian plum tomatoes, coarsely chopped
$1^1/_4$ tablespoons oregano
1 tablespoon chili powder
2 teaspoons cumin
1 teaspoon cayenne pepper
1 cup drained canned kidney beans
1 cup drained canned chick-peas
1 cup drained canned cannellini beans
8 ounces snow peas, thickly sliced

Sauté the bell peppers in 2 teaspoons of the olive oil in a skillet for 2 to 3 minutes or until tender. Add the corn, salt and pepper and mix well.

Cook the onions, garlic and undrained tomatoes in the remaining $^1/_3$ cup olive oil in a large saucepan over medium heat until the onions are tender. Stir in the oregano, chili powder, cumin and cayenne pepper. Add the bell pepper mixture, kidney beans, chick-peas, cannellini beans and snow peas and mix well. Cook just until heated through. Ladle into soup bowls. Serve with corn bread.

Yield: 8 servings

Asparagus Salad with Lemon Soy Dressing

1¼ pounds asparagus spears, diagonally cut into ½-inch pieces
8 scallions
1 tablespoon olive oil
¼ teaspoon minced gingerroot
5 scallions, minced
½ cup reduced-sodium chicken bouillon
1 tablespoon cider vinegar
1 teaspoon soy sauce
½ teaspoon sugar
⅛ to ¼ teaspoon pepper
Lemon juice to taste

Steam the asparagus and 8 whole scallions in a steamer over boiling water for 5 minutes or until tender-crisp. Remove the vegetables to a colander. Rinse with cold water; drain. Chill, covered, until cool.

Heat the olive oil in a saucepan over medium-high heat until hot. Add the gingerroot. Sauté until it begins to color. Stir in 2 of the minced scallions. Sauté for several seconds. Add the bouillon, vinegar, soy sauce and sugar and mix well. Bring to a boil over medium-high heat, stirring frequently. Boil for 30 seconds. Stir in the pepper and lemon juice.

Combine the asparagus, whole scallions and remaining 3 minced scallions in a bowl and toss gently. Drizzle with the dressing and toss to coat.

Yield: 4 servings

MARINATED BEAN AND RICE SALAD

3 (16-ounce) cans black beans, drained, rinsed
3 cups cooked brown rice
1 onion, finely chopped
$^1/_2$ cup chopped green bell pepper
$^1/_2$ cup chopped red bell pepper
$^1/_4$ cup chopped fresh cilantro
3 tablespoons red wine vinegar
3 tablespoons corn oil
3 tablespoons vegetable broth
2 teaspoons chopped fresh thyme
2 garlic cloves, minced
$^1/_2$ teaspoon pepper

Combine the beans, brown rice, onion, green bell pepper and red bell pepper in a bowl and toss gently.

Whisk the cilantro, wine vinegar, corn oil, broth, thyme, garlic and pepper in a bowl. Add to the bean mixture and toss gently. Marinate, covered, in the refrigerator for 2 to 4 hours.

YIELD: 12 SERVINGS

LIGHTEN UP

Decrease the sodium by substituting 1 to 1$^1/_4$ pounds cooked dried black beans for the canned black beans.

Roasted Garlic Caesar Salad

Recipe for Caesar Croutons

Heat 3 tablespoons olive oil and 3 tablespoons butter in a skillet over medium-high heat until hot. Add 3 cups dry bread cubes and toss to coat. Reduce the heat to medium-low. Stir in 2 large minced garlic cloves and 1 teaspoon each chopped fresh chives, tarragon and parsley. Cook for 20 minutes or until the bread cubes are brown, stirring frequently. Spoon into a bowl. Add 3 tablespoons freshly grated Parmesan cheese and toss to coat. Spread on a baking sheet. Let stand until cool. Store in an airtight container.

2 large garlic bulbs
1/4 cup dry vermouth
1/3 cup plus 1 tablespoon olive oil
Pepper to taste
2 tablespoons fresh lemon juice
1 tablespoon red wine vinegar
1 tablespoon anchovy paste
1 teaspoon Dijon mustard
1 teaspoon Worcestershire sauce
1/8 teaspoon Tabasco sauce
2 large heads romaine, torn into bite-size pieces
1 1/4 cups freshly grated Parmesan cheese
1 recipe Caesar Croutons (in sidebar)

Peel off the papery outer skin of the garlic, leaving the bulbs intact. Arrange in a small baking dish. Pour the vermouth over the garlic. Drizzle with 1 tablespoon of the olive oil. Sprinkle with pepper. Roast, covered with foil, at 300 degrees for 1 1/2 hours or until the garlic is very soft. Let stand until cool.

Squeeze the garlic to remove the cloves from the skins and place in a bowl. Mash with a fork until of a paste consistency. Spoon into a blender container. Add the lemon juice, wine vinegar, anchovy paste, Dijon mustard, Worcestershire sauce and Tabasco sauce. Add the remaining 1/3 cup olive oil in a fine stream, processing constantly until smooth. Let stand, covered, at room temperature for up to 2 hours.

Toss the romaine and dressing in a bowl until coated. Add the cheese and croutons and toss to mix. Season with pepper. Serve immediately. Top with grilled shrimp, grilled chicken or tenderloin for an entrée.

Yield: 8 servings

GRILLED EGGPLANT SALAD

2 small eggplant, peeled
1 tablespoon salt
1 cup olive oil
3 tomatoes, sliced
1 cup shredded mozzarella cheese
$1/2$ cup kalamata olives
2 tablespoons capers
2 to 4 tablespoons green olive oil
Wine vinegar to taste
Salt and freshly ground pepper to taste
5 fresh basil leaves, julienned

LIGHTEN UP

Omit 1 cup olive oil and spray the eggplant slices heavily with nonstick olive oil cooking spray. Substitute part-skim mozzarella cheese for the mozzarella cheese.

Cut the eggplant into 1-inch slices. Sprinkle with 1 tablespoon salt. Place in a colander. Let stand for 20 minutes. Rinse the eggplant and pat dry. Arrange in a shallow dish. Pour 1 cup olive oil over the eggplant and toss to coat. Let stand for 10 minutes; drain.

Grill the eggplant over hot coals until brown on both sides. Layer the eggplant and tomato slices on a serving platter. Sprinkle with the cheese, olives and capers. Drizzle with the green olive oil and wine vinegar. Sprinkle with salt and pepper to taste. Top with the basil.

YIELD: 6 SERVINGS

MIDDLE EASTERN CARROT SLAW

$1/2$ to $2/3$ cup reduced-fat sour cream
1 teaspoon cumin
$1/2$ teaspoon coriander
$1/8$ teaspoon cayenne pepper
3 cups coarsely shredded carrots
$1/4$ cup chopped fresh cilantro

Combine $1/2$ cup sour cream, cumin, coriander and cayenne pepper in a bowl and mix well. Stir in the carrots and cilantro, adding additional sour cream if needed. Chill, covered, until serving time.

YIELD: 6 SERVINGS

BABY GREENS WITH RED POTATOES AND WILD MUSHROOMS

BACON SALAD DRESSING

4 ounces bacon, coarsely chopped
1 cup plus 1 tablespoon olive oil
$2/3$ cup chopped shallots
$1^1/2$ teaspoons thyme
$1/4$ cup white wine vinegar
$1/8$ teaspoon saffron
$1/4$ cup chopped fresh tarragon
Salt and pepper to taste

SALAD

8 small red potatoes
8 ounces each shiitake and oyster mushrooms
Salt and pepper to taste
12 ounces green beans, trimmed
16 cups assorted baby salad greens
2 large heads Belgian endive, sliced

To prepare the dressing, fry the bacon in a skillet until crisp. Drain, reserving the pan drippings. Combine the reserved pan drippings, 1 tablespoon of the olive oil, shallots and thyme in the skillet. Sauté for 2 minutes. Stir in the wine vinegar and saffron. Remove from heat. Whisk in the remaining 1 cup olive oil and tarragon. Season with salt and pepper.

To prepare the salad, cut each potato into 6 wedges. Place in a bowl. Combine the shiitake mushrooms and oyster mushrooms in a separate bowl. Pour $1/4$ of the dressing over the potatoes and $1/4$ of the dressing over the mushrooms and toss to coat. Season the potatoes and mushrooms with salt and pepper.

Arrange the potatoes and mushrooms in single layers on 2 separate baking sheets. Marinate for 30 minutes. Roast the potatoes at 400 degrees for 40 minutes or until brown and crisp, turning once. Roast the mushrooms at 400 degrees for 15 minutes or until brown and crisp, turning once. Cook the green beans in boiling water in a saucepan for 4 minutes or until tender-crisp; drain. Rinse with cold water; drain.

Combine the potatoes, mushrooms, green beans, salad greens and endive in a bowl and toss to mix. Drizzle with the remaining dressing and mix well. Sprinkle with the bacon. Serve immediately.

YIELD: 16 SERVINGS

FIELD GREENS WITH ROSEMARY VINAIGRETTE

ROSEMARY VINAIGRETTE

1 cup rice wine vinegar
1/4 cup corn oil
Juice of 1/2 lemon
2 teaspoons white Worcestershire sauce
3/4 to 1 cup snipped fresh rosemary
3 shallots, chopped

SALAD

6 heads mâche
2 heads frisée
1 head radicchio
2 bunches watercress
2 bunches arugula
6 ounces mozzarella cheese, sliced
1 large tomato, sliced

To prepare the vinaigrette, combine the rice wine vinegar, corn oil, lemon juice, Worcestershire sauce, rosemary and shallots in a jar with a tight-fitting lid. Cover the jar and shake to mix. Store any leftovers in the refrigerator.

To prepare the salad, tear the mâche, frisée, radicchio, watercress and arugula into bite-size pieces. Toss in a bowl. Add the desired amount of vinaigrette and toss to coat. Spoon the greens evenly onto 12 chilled salad plates. Arrange the mozzarella slices over the tomato slices and arrange over the greens. Serve immediately.

YIELD: 12 SERVINGS

GREEK TORTELLINI SALAD

MINT SALAD DRESSING

1/2 cup white vinegar
1/2 cup olive oil
3 tablespoons fresh lemon juice
2 tablespoons dry sherry
3 tablespoons chopped fresh mint
1 1/2 teaspoons seasoned salt
1 teaspoon garlic powder
1 teaspoon black pepper
1/4 teaspoon red pepper flakes

SALAD

2 (9-ounce) packages fresh cheese tortellini
1 red bell pepper, julienned
1 green bell pepper, julienned
1 yellow bell pepper, julienned
1 small red onion, thinly sliced
1/4 cup sliced Greek olives
3/4 cup crumbled feta cheese

To prepare the dressing, combine the vinegar, olive oil, lemon juice and sherry in a jar with a tight-fitting lid. Cover the jar and shake to mix. Add the mint, seasoned salt, garlic powder, black pepper and red pepper flakes. Shake to mix.

To prepare the salad, cook the pasta using package directions, omitting the salt and fat; drain. Combine the pasta, bell peppers, onion and olives in a bowl and toss gently to mix. Add the dressing and mix well. Chill, covered, for 8 to 10 hours. Add the feta cheese just before serving and toss to mix.

YIELD: 8 SERVINGS

Shrimp and Orzo Salad

Orange Vinaigrette

1 cup fresh orange juice
6 tablespoons olive oil
2 to 3 tablespoons mixed minced fresh herbs
4 teaspoons balsamic vinegar
$3/4$ teaspoon salt
$1/8$ teaspoon cayenne pepper

Pasta and Shrimp

1 cup orzo
2 tablespoons olive oil
2 pounds large shrimp, peeled, deveined
Salt and cayenne pepper to taste
2 heads red leaf lettuce, torn into bite-size pieces
5 bunches arugula
$1/2$ cup mixed minced fresh herbs
$1/4$ red onion, thinly sliced
Sections of 3 large oranges

To prepare the vinaigrette, whisk the orange juice, olive oil, fresh herbs, balsamic vinegar, salt and cayenne pepper in a bowl until mixed.

To prepare the pasta and shrimp, cook the pasta using package directions, omitting the salt and fat; drain. Let stand until cool. Combine the pasta with $2^1/2$ tablespoons of the vinaigrette and toss to coat. Heat 1 tablespoon of the olive oil in a skillet over medium-high heat until hot. Add half the shrimp. Sauté for 1 minute or until the shrimp turn pink. Season with salt and cayenne pepper. Remove to a platter. Repeat the process with the remaining olive oil and shrimp. Combine the shrimp with $1/4$ cup of the vinaigrette in a bowl and mix well. Marinate at room temperature for 20 to 30 minutes, stirring several times.

Combine the leaf lettuce, arugula, fresh herbs and onion in a bowl. Reserve $1/4$ cup of the remaining vinaigrette. Add the remaining vinaigrette to the greens and toss lightly. Spoon the mixed green mixture onto each of 4 serving plates. Place a mound of the pasta beside the greens. Top with the shrimp and orange sections. Drizzle each serving with 1 tablespoon of the reserved vinaigrette.

Yield: 4 servings

WILD RICE AND WALNUT SALAD

8 ounces wild rice
1 cup dried cranberries
1 cup chopped walnuts
1/2 cup orange juice
Grated zest of 1 large orange
4 green onions, finely chopped
1/4 cup olive oil
1 1/2 teaspoons salt

Cook the wild rice using package directions, omitting the salt and fat. Let stand until cool. Combine the wild rice, cranberries, walnuts, orange juice, zest and green onions in a bowl and mix gently. Add the olive oil and salt and toss to mix.

YIELD: 8 SERVINGS

TOMATO, GREEN BEAN AND BASIL SALAD

8 ounces fresh green beans, trimmed
4 large ripe tomatoes, cut into 1/4-inch slices
1/2 cup raspberry vinegar
1/2 cup walnut oil
Salt and pepper to taste
1/3 cup chopped walnuts, toasted
1 bunch basil, julienned

Blanch the green beans in boiling water in a saucepan; drain. Plunge into ice water to stop the cooking process; drain. Arrange the green beans and tomatoes on a serving platter. Whisk the raspberry vinegar, walnut oil, salt and pepper in a bowl until blended. Drizzle over the salad. Sprinkle with the walnuts and basil. Serve immediately.

YIELD: 8 SERVINGS

GRILLED TUNA SALAD NIÇOISE

BALSAMIC VINAIGRETTE

1/4 cup olive oil
2 tablespoons balsamic vinegar
2 tablespoons finely minced fresh rosemary
1 tablespoon wine
2 garlic cloves, finely chopped
1/4 teaspoon pepper

SALAD

1 pound fresh green beans, trimmed
8 small red potatoes
8 plum tomatoes, cut into quarters
1/4 cup black olives
4 (6-ounce) tuna steaks, 1 inch thick
1 teaspoon lemon pepper
6 cups mixed baby greens
1/2 small red onion, thinly sliced
2 tablespoons minced fresh parsley

To prepare the vinaigrette, whisk the olive oil, balsamic vinegar, rosemary, wine, garlic and pepper in a bowl until mixed.

To prepare the salad, break the beans into bite-size pieces. Combine with a small amount of water in a microwave-safe dish. Microwave, covered, on High for 8 to 10 minutes or until tender-crisp; drain. Prick the potatoes with a fork. Combine with a small amount of water in a microwave-safe dish. Microwave on High for 10 minutes or until tender; drain. Toss the potatoes and green beans in a bowl. Let stand until cool. Add the tomatoes and olives and mix gently. Pour half the vinaigrette over the potato mixture and toss to coat. Marinate at room temperature for 30 minutes.

Sprinkle both sides of the tuna with lemon pepper. Arrange the tuna on a grill rack sprayed with nonstick cooking spray. Grill over hot coals for 3 to 5 minutes or until the edges of the steaks begin to turn white; turn. Grill for 3 minutes longer for medium or for 5 minutes longer for well done.

Arrange the mixed greens evenly on each of 4 serving plates. Spoon 1/4 of the vegetable mixture along the side of each plate. Arrange the onion over the mixed greens. Top with the tuna steaks. Sprinkle with the parsley. Drizzle with the remaining vinaigrette.

YIELD: 4 SERVINGS

GRILLED BEEF TENDERLOIN WITH FRESH HERBS

TARRAGON BUTTER

3/4 cup (1 1/2 sticks) butter, softened
3 tablespoons chopped fresh tarragon
3 tablespoons chopped fresh parsley
Juice of 2 large lemons
Salt and white pepper to taste

BEEF

3 cups red wine
1/3 cup olive oil
1 large onion, finely chopped
1/4 cup chopped fresh parsley
3 garlic cloves, crushed
1 tablespoon chopped fresh rosemary
3/4 teaspoon salt
1/2 teaspoon freshly ground pepper
1/2 teaspoon oregano
1 (3- to 4-pound) beef tenderloin

To prepare the butter, combine the butter, tarragon, parsley, lemon juice, salt and white pepper in a bowl and mix well. Shape into a 1-inch roll. Chill, wrapped in plastic wrap, until firm.

To prepare the beef, whisk the wine, olive oil, onion, parsley, garlic, rosemary, salt, pepper and oregano in a bowl. Pour over the beef in a sealable plastic bag; seal tightly. Marinate in the refrigerator for 4 to 10 hours, turning occasionally. Drain and pat dry, discarding the marinade. Arrange the beef on a greased grill rack 5 to 6 inches above the heat source. Grill for 20 to 25 minutes, turning frequently. Close the lid and vent halfway. Grill until a meat thermometer registers 130 degrees for rare or 140 degrees for medium. Let stand for several minutes before serving. Slice and arrange on a serving platter. Serve with the butter.

YIELD: 8 SERVINGS

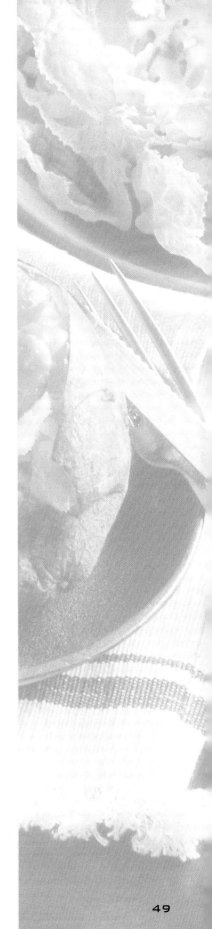

FLANK STEAK WITH PARMESAN RICE FILLING

1 (2-pound) flank steak
$^1/_2$ cup finely chopped onion
$^1/_4$ cup ($^1/_2$ stick) butter or margarine
1$^1/_2$ cups cooked rice
$^1/_2$ cup plus 2 tablespoons chopped fresh parsley
$^1/_3$ cup freshly grated Parmesan cheese
$^1/_2$ teaspoon salt
$^1/_4$ teaspoon pepper
1 beef bouillon cube
1 cup hot water
1 tablespoon sugar
$^1/_2$ teaspoon thyme

Cut a pocket horizontally in the side of the steak with a sharp knife. Sauté the onion in the butter in a skillet until brown. Stir in the rice, $^1/_2$ cup of the parsley, cheese, salt and pepper. Spoon the rice mixture into the pocket. Secure with wooden picks. Arrange the steak in a baking pan.

Dissolve the bouillon in the hot water in a bowl. Stir in the remaining 2 tablespoons parsley, sugar and thyme. Pour over the steak. Bake, covered, at 350 degrees for 1$^1/_2$ hours or until of the desired degree of doneness. Discard the wooden picks. Slice as desired.

YIELD: 6 SERVINGS

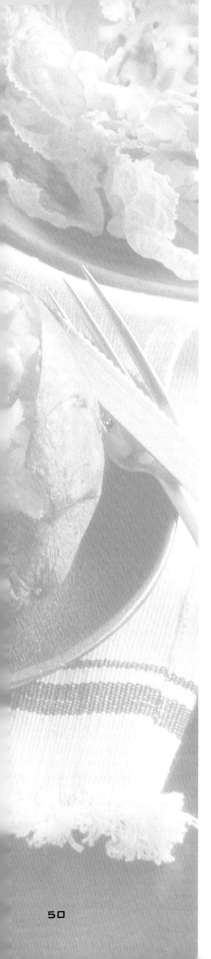

Beef Tournedos with Wild Mushroom Sauté

4 (6-ounce) beef tenderloin steaks, 1 inch thick, trimmed
6 ounces fresh wild mushrooms, coarsely chopped
1 shallot, finely chopped
1 tablespoon chopped fresh oregano
3 tablespoons butter or margarine
Salt and pepper to taste
1/2 cup cabernet sauvignon
1/2 cup beef stock

Cut a horizontal pocket in the side of each steak. Sauté the mushrooms, shallot and oregano in 1 tablespoon of the butter in a skillet for 2 minutes or until the vegetables are tender. Spoon the mushroom mixture into the pockets. Secure with wooden picks.

Heat a nonstick skillet over medium heat until hot. Add the steaks. Cook for 3 minutes on each side or until medium-rare. Remove the steaks to a heated platter with a slotted spoon, reserving the pan drippings. Sprinkle with salt and pepper. Discard the wooden picks.

Stir the wine into the reserved pan drippings. Cook over high heat for 1 minute, stirring constantly. Stir in the stock. Cook until reduced to 1/4 cup, stirring frequently. Whisk in the remaining 2 tablespoons butter. Drizzle over the steaks. Serve immediately.

Yield: 4 servings

STUFFED BEEF FILLETS WITH MARSALA SAUCE

8 (6-ounce) beef tenderloin steaks
1 (10-ounce) package frozen chopped spinach, thawed, drained
1/2 cup crumbled bleu cheese
2 tablespoons prepared horseradish
1/4 teaspoon pepper
8 slices bacon
1/4 cup olive oil
1/2 cup marsala
1/2 cup dry red wine
1 1/2 teaspoons minced garlic
1/4 teaspoon Tabasco sauce
1 tablespoon water
1 tablespoon tomato paste
Sprigs of parsley

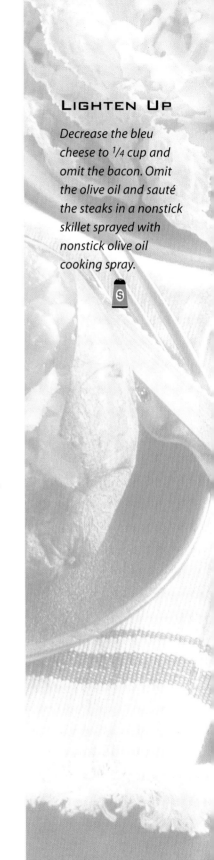

LIGHTEN UP

Decrease the bleu cheese to 1/4 cup and omit the bacon. Omit the olive oil and sauté the steaks in a nonstick skillet sprayed with nonstick olive oil cooking spray.

Cut a pocket horizontally in the side of each steak with a sharp knife. Press the excess moisture from the spinach. Combine the spinach, bleu cheese, horseradish and pepper in a bowl and mix well. Spoon the spinach mixture into the pockets. Wrap each steak with 1 slice of the bacon to close the opening. Secure with wooden picks.

Cook the steaks in the olive oil in a skillet over medium-high heat for 3 minutes per side for rare or 5 minutes per side for medium, turning once. Remove the steaks to a heated platter with a slotted spoon, reserving the pan drippings. Add the marsala and red wine to the reserved pan drippings, stirring to deglaze the skillet. Stir in the garlic. Cook for several seconds. Add the Tabasco sauce and a mixture of the water and tomato paste and mix well; reduce heat.

Cook for 1 minute, stirring constantly. Return the steaks to the skillet, turning to coat. Remove the steaks to a serving platter with a slotted spoon. Drizzle with the sauce. Top with the parsley. Serve immediately.

YIELD: 8 SERVINGS

SPICY BEEF AND POLENTA

LIGHTEN UP

Decrease the fat grams by substituting skim milk for the whole milk and ground turkey for the ground round.

1 large green bell pepper, chopped
1 large onion, finely chopped
2 pounds ground round
2 cups milk
1 cup (scant) cornmeal
1 (16-ounce) can whole kernel corn, drained
1 teaspoon chili powder
1/2 cup shredded Cheddar cheese
Salt and pepper to taste

Spray a nonstick skillet with nonstick cooking spray and heat until hot. Add the bell pepper and onion. Sauté until the vegetables are tender. Add the ground round. Cook until the ground round is brown and crumbly, stirring constantly; drain. Stir in the milk and cornmeal. Cook until thickened, stirring constantly. Remove from heat.

Add the corn, chili powder, cheese, salt and pepper to the ground round mixture and mix well. Spoon into a 9x13-inch baking dish. Bake at 350 degrees for 50 minutes or until brown and bubbly.

YIELD: 8 SERVINGS

EGGPLANT PARMESAN AND BEEF CASSEROLE

1 pound lean ground beef
$^1/_2$ cup chopped onion
1 garlic clove, minced
1 (16-ounce) can Italian tomatoes
1 cup plus 1 tablespoon water
1 (6-ounce) can tomato paste
1 tablespoon sugar
2 teaspoons oregano
1 teaspoon basil
1$^1/_2$ teaspoons salt
$^1/_4$ teaspoon pepper
2 eggs
1 unpeeled large eggplant, cut into $^1/_2$-inch slices
$^1/_2$ cup dry bread crumbs
$^1/_4$ cup vegetable oil
1$^1/_4$ cups freshly grated Parmesan cheese
8 ounces mozzarella cheese, shredded

Brown the ground beef with the onion and garlic in a skillet, stirring until the ground beef is crumbly; drain. Stir in the undrained tomatoes, 1 cup of the water, tomato paste, sugar, oregano, basil, salt and pepper. Simmer for 20 minutes, stirring occasionally.

Whisk the eggs and the remaining 1 tablespoon water in a bowl. Dip the eggplant into the egg mixture and coat with the bread crumbs. Fry the eggplant in the oil in a skillet until brown on both sides; drain.

Layer the eggplant, Parmesan cheese, mozzarella cheese and ground beef mixture $^1/_2$ at a time in a greased 2-quart baking dish. Bake at 325 degrees for 40 to 45 minutes or until bubbly. Serve with a tossed green salad and crusty French bread.

YIELD: 6 SERVINGS

LIGHTEN UP

Substitute ground turkey for the ground beef, no-added-salt tomatoes for the Italian tomatoes, 4 egg whites for the 2 eggs and part-skim mozzarella cheese for the mozzarella cheese. Omit the oil and spray the eggplant slices heavily with nonstick olive oil cooking spray. Bake until brown on both sides. If you prefer to use ground beef, after browning place the ground beef in a colander and rinse with hot water. This will further reduce the fat content.

BOURBON-GLAZED CORNED BEEF

1 (6- to 7-pound) corned beef
3/4 cup blended bourbon
2 bay leaves
2 garlic cloves
4 white peppercorns
4 whole cloves
3/4 cup packed brown sugar
1/4 cup orange juice
1 teaspoon prepared mustard
1 large head green cabbage, cut into wedges

Combine the corned beef with enough water to cover in a Dutch oven. Add 1/2 cup of the bourbon, bay leaves, garlic, peppercorns and cloves. Bring to a boil; reduce heat. Simmer, covered, for 3 to 4 hours or until tender. Remove the corned beef to a baking pan. Cut the outer fat in a crisscross pattern. Strain the pan juices and return the liquid to the saucepan, discarding the solids.

Combine 2 tablespoons of the reserved corned beef liquid, remaining 1/4 cup bourbon, brown sugar, orange juice and prepared mustard in a small saucepan. Cook over low heat until blended, stirring frequently. Pour over the corned beef. Bake at 400 degrees for 30 minutes, basting every 10 minutes.

Add the cabbage to the reserved corned beef liquid in the saucepan. Bring to a simmer. Simmer for 10 minutes or until tender. Serve with the corned beef.

YIELD: 10 SERVINGS

VEAL ROAST WITH PEAR SALSA

PEAR SALSA

$1^1/2$ cups finely chopped unpeeled pear
1 cup finely chopped green bell pepper
1 cup finely chopped red bell pepper
$1/2$ cup finely chopped fresh parsley
$1/4$ cup finely chopped red onion
2 jalapeño chiles, seeded, finely chopped
2 tablespoons lemon juice
1 tablespoon finely chopped fresh chives
1 tablespoon finely chopped fresh tarragon
1 tablespoon red wine vinegar

VEAL

1 ($3^1/2$-pound) rolled boneless veal rump roast
1 garlic clove, cut into halves
1 teaspoon cracked pepper
1 teaspoon vegetable oil
$3/4$ cup dry white wine
$1/2$ teaspoon beef bouillon granules

To prepare the salsa, combine the pear, bell peppers, parsley, onion, jalapeño chiles, lemon juice, chives, tarragon and wine vinegar in a bowl and mix well. Chill, covered, for 8 hours or longer.

To prepare the veal, unroll the roast and trim the excess fat. Rub the cut sides of the garlic over the surface of the veal. Reroll and tie at 2-inch intervals with kitchen twine. Sprinkle with the pepper.

Spray a Dutch oven with nonstick cooking spray. Add the oil. Heat over medium-high heat until hot. Add the veal. Cook until brown on all sides, turning frequently. Add the wine and bouillon granules. Roast, covered, at 325 degrees for $1^1/2$ hours, basting frequently. Remove to a serving platter; discard the twine. Slice and serve with the salsa.

YIELD: 14 SERVINGS

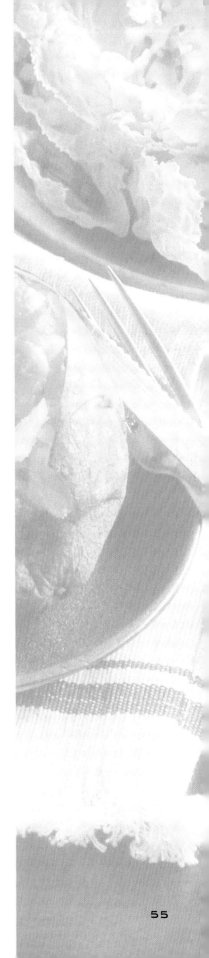

GRILLED VEAL WITH RUM SAUCE

4 (8-ounce) veal loin chops
1/2 cup dark rum
1/4 cup olive oil
1/3 cup fresh lime juice
2 shallots, chopped
1 tablespoon chopped fresh thyme
1 teaspoon angostura bitters
1/4 cup honey
2 teaspoons thick hot pepper sauce
6 tablespoons butter or margarine
Salt to taste

*Arrange the veal chops in a single layer in a baking pan. Whisk the rum,
olive oil, lime juice, shallots, thyme, bitters, honey and pepper sauce in a
bowl until mixed. Pour over the veal chops. Let stand at room temperature
for 1 hour, turning once. You may marinate the veal chops for a longer
period in the refrigerator. Drain, reserving the marinade.*

*Grill the veal chops over hot coals until cooked through. Remove to a
platter and cover to keep warm. Bring the reserved marinade to a boil in a
saucepan. Boil for 5 minutes. Add the butter gradually, whisking
constantly. Cook until blended and heated through, stirring constantly.
Season with salt. Serve with the veal chops.*

YIELD: 4 SERVINGS

Pecan-Crusted Rack of Lamb

2 (2^1/2-pound) racks of lamb or loin chops, trimmed
^{1}/2 cup mushrooms with stems
^{1}/2 cup chopped fresh parsley
1 carrot, chopped
1 stalk celery, chopped
^{1}/2 small onion, chopped
2 teaspoons minced fresh rosemary
2 teaspoons minced fresh tarragon
1 teaspoon minced shallot
1 teaspoon minced garlic
2 bay leaves, crushed
6 tablespoons unsalted butter or margarine
4 cups beef broth or lamb stock
2 cups cabernet sauvignon
2 tablespoons tomato paste
1 medium tomato, crushed
2 tablespoons flour
1 tablespoon barbecue sauce
^{1}/2 teaspoon sugar
Salt and pepper to taste
Pecan Coating (in sidebar)

Rx Recipe for Pecan Coating

Sauté 2 teaspoons minced fresh rosemary and 1 minced garlic clove in ^{1}/4 cup butter in a skillet over medium heat for 1 minute. Stir in ^{1}/2 cup ground toasted pecans and ^{1}/2 cup coarsely ground toasted bread crumbs. Sauté for 5 minutes or until light brown and crisp. Season with salt and pepper. Remove from heat and cover.

Divide each rack of lamb crosswise into halves. Grill over hot coals for 8 minutes or until seared on all sides. Remove to a baking pan. Bake at 400 degrees for 12 minutes or until of the desired degree of doneness.

Sauté the mushrooms, parsley, carrot, celery, onion, rosemary, tarragon, shallot, garlic and bay leaves in 4 tablespoons of the butter in a skillet for 2 minutes. Stir in the next 4 ingredients. Boil for 20 minutes or until reduced by ^{1}/2, stirring occasionally.

Combine the remaining 2 tablespoons butter and flour in a saucepan. Cook over medium heat until the roux is light brown, stirring constantly. Stir the roux and barbecue sauce into the wine sauce. Simmer for 15 minutes. Strain, discarding the solids. Stir in the sugar and season with salt and pepper.

Spread the Pecan Coating on a platter. Brush the lamb with some of the sauce and roll each half rack in the coating to form a crust. Slice the racks into chops. Arrange on a serving platter. Spoon the remaining wine sauce over the chops. Serve immediately.

Yield: 4 servings

Roast Lamb with Potato and Tomato au Jus

1 garlic clove, cut into halves
2 pounds baking potatoes, peeled, sliced
5 large tomatoes, sliced
2 large onions, thinly sliced
Coarse salt and freshly ground pepper to taste
2 teaspoons fresh thyme leaves
6 garlic cloves, finely chopped
2/3 cup dry white wine
1/3 cup olive oil
1 (6- to 7-pound) leg of lamb, trimmed

Rub the inside of a 10x16-inch oval roasting pan with the cut sides of 1 garlic clove. Layer the potatoes, tomatoes and onions in the prepared pan, sprinkling each layer evenly with salt, pepper, thyme and finely chopped garlic. Pour the wine and olive oil over the prepared layers.

Season the lamb with salt and pepper. Place the roasting pan in the oven. Lay a wire rack over the top of the pan. Arrange the lamb on the rack so the juices will drip into the vegetables.

Roast at 400 degrees for 1 3/4 hours; do not turn the lamb. Remove just the lamb from the oven to a heated serving platter. Let stand for 20 minutes before carving. Turn off the oven. Let the gratin stand in the oven with the door ajar until serving time. Carve the lamb and arrange on a heated platter. Serve with the gratin.

Yield: 10 servings

PORK LOIN WITH RED ONIONS AND CRANBERRIES

4 (6-ounce) slices pork loin, $3/4$ inch thick
1$1/4$ teaspoons thyme
Salt and pepper to taste
3 tablespoons flour
5 teaspoons butter or margarine
2 teaspoons corn oil
2 small red onions, thinly sliced
1 cup apple juice
1$1/2$ cups cranberries
$1/2$ cup chicken stock

Rub both sides of the pork with the thyme, salt and pepper. Coat with the flour. Heat 2 teaspoons of the butter and corn oil in a skillet over medium-high heat until the butter melts. Add the pork. Cook for 2 minutes per side or until brown. Remove the pork to a heated platter.

Wipe the skillet clean with paper towels. Add the remaining 3 teaspoons butter. Heat until melted. Add the onions. Sauté until golden brown. Stir in the apple juice. Bring to a boil. Stir in the cranberries and stock. Bring to a boil; reduce heat. Return the pork to the skillet.

Simmer until the pork is cooked through, stirring occasionally. Remove the pork to 4 heated dinner plates with a slotted spoon. Increase the heat. Bring the sauce to a boil. Boil for 2 minutes or until thickened, stirring constantly. Drizzle over the pork.

YIELD: 4 SERVINGS

SPICE ROAD STUFFED PORK LOIN

3/4 cup chopped prunes
3/4 cup chopped dried apricots
1 tablespoon grated gingerroot
1 teaspoon grated orange zest
1/2 teaspoon cinnamon
1 1/2 teaspoons cumin
Salt and pepper to taste
1 (4-pound) pork loin roast, butterflied
1/4 cup packed brown sugar
2 teaspoons cider vinegar
2 teaspoons flour
1 teaspoon dry mustard
1/2 cup water
1 teaspoon cornstarch

Combine the prunes, apricots, gingerroot, zest, cinnamon, 1/2 teaspoon of the cumin, salt and pepper in a bowl and mix well. Open the pork roast flat, book-style and place on a hard surface. Spoon the prune mixture down the center. Tie into a roll at 2-inch intervals with kitchen twine. Place in a roasting pan.

Combine the brown sugar, vinegar, flour, dry mustard and remaining 1 teaspoon cumin in a bowl and mix well. Spread over the roast. Bake at 325 degrees for 1 1/2 hours or until of the desired degree of doneness, basting occasionally. Remove the roast to a heated platter with a slotted spoon, reserving the pan juices.

Skim the pan juices. Add the water, stirring to deglaze the pan. Stir in a mixture of the cornstarch and a small amount of cold water. Cook for 1 minute or until thickened, stirring constantly. Serve with the pork.

YIELD: 8 SERVINGS

RASPBERRY SAGE PORK CHOPS

1 tablespoon butter or margarine
1 tablespoon olive oil
8 (6-ounce) pork chops, 1 inch thick
$1/2$ cup raspberry vinegar
2 large garlic cloves, minced
$1/2$ cup chicken broth
2 tomatoes, chopped
1 tablespoon chopped fresh parsley
1 teaspoon sage
Salt and pepper to taste
$1/2$ cup fresh raspberries
Fresh sage leaves

Heat the butter and olive oil in a skillet until the butter melts. Add the pork chops. Cook over medium-high heat until brown on both sides; drain. Reduce the heat to medium-low. Add 2 tablespoons of the raspberry vinegar and garlic. Simmer, covered, for 10 minutes. Remove the pork chops to a platter with a slotted spoon, reserving the pan juices. Cover the pork chops to keep warm.

Add the remaining raspberry vinegar to the reserved pan juices and stir to deglaze the skillet. Bring to a boil. Boil until of the consistency of a thick glaze, stirring frequently. Add the broth, tomatoes, parsley and 1 teaspoon sage and mix gently. Bring to a boil.

Boil until reduced by half, stirring frequently; strain. Season with salt and pepper. Spoon over the pork chops. Top with the raspberries and sage leaves.

YIELD: 8 SERVINGS

CLASSIC HERB-ROASTED CHICKEN

1 (4- to 5-pound) roasting chicken
2 tablespoons fresh lemon juice
Salt and freshly ground pepper to taste
1 apple, cut into quarters
1 onion, cut into quarters
1 stalk celery, coarsely chopped
12 sprigs of thyme, minced
8 sprigs of rosemary, minced
8 fresh sage leaves, minced
16 shallots, trimmed
4 unpeeled large garlic cloves
3/4 cup white wine

Rub the chicken cavity with the lemon juice, salt and pepper. Place the apple, onion, celery and 3/4 of the fresh herbs in the cavity; truss. Place the chicken breast side up in a roasting pan. Roast at 400 degrees for 15 minutes.

Arrange the shallots and garlic around the chicken. Reserve a small amount of the remaining fresh herbs for the garnish. Sprinkle the remaining herbs around the chicken. Pour the wine over the chicken.

Roast for 1 to 1 1/2 hours longer or until the juices run clear when the chicken is pierced with a fork. Arrange the chicken on a serving platter surrounded by the shallots and garlic. Sprinkle with the reserved herbs.

YIELD: 5 SERVINGS

Rx FACTS ABOUT POISON PREVENTION

* Never tell children that their medicine "tastes good like candy."

* Always be sure to purchase child-resistant containers and recap correctly after each use.

* All household cleaners, medications, etc. should be stored out of reach of children even if they have a child-resistant cap.

* Read the warning labels printed on products and take them seriously.

CALYPSO CHICKEN BREASTS

$1/2$ teaspoon cumin
$1/2$ teaspoon coriander
$1/4$ teaspoon ginger
$1/8$ teaspoon cayenne pepper
4 boneless skinless chicken breasts
1 tablespoon corn oil
$1/4$ cup fresh lemon juice
3 tablespoons fresh orange juice
3 tablespoons fresh lime juice
$1/3$ cup mango chutney
Sprigs of cilantro

Combine the cumin, coriander, ginger and cayenne pepper in a small bowl and mix well. Rub the herb mixture over the surface of the chicken. Heat the corn oil in a nonstick skillet over medium heat. Add the chicken.
   Cook for 10 to 15 minutes or until cooked through, turning occasionally. Remove the chicken to a platter with a slotted spoon, reserving the pan juices. Cover the chicken to keep warm. Stir the lemon juice, orange juice, lime juice and chutney into the pan juices. Bring to a boil. Boil for 2 minutes or until thickened, stirring constantly. Drizzle over the chicken. Top with sprigs of cilantro.

YIELD: 4 SERVINGS

Rx FACTS ABOUT WHAT TO DO IN A POISON EMERGENCY

✳ Contact the nearest Poison Prevention Center if any household or toxic substance has been ingested or spilled onto the skin or in the eyes. If your child has convulsions or is unconscious call 911 first.

✳ Syrup of Ipecac is a medicine used to induce vomiting. Keeping a bottle on hand is a good idea. Depending on the situation, the Poison Prevention Center may instruct you to administer Ipecac.

✳ Do not induce vomiting unless instructed by the Poison Prevention Center or your physician.

CHICKEN VERONIQUE

3 tablespoons dry bread crumbs
$1/2$ teaspoon tarragon
$1/8$ teaspoon pepper
4 boneless skinless chicken breasts
2 tablespoons butter or margarine
4 ounces fresh mushrooms, sliced
$1/2$ cup chopped onion
2 tablespoons dry white wine
1 chicken bouillon cube
2 tablespoons water
1 cup seedless green grapes
2 cups cooked wild rice

Combine the bread crumbs, tarragon and pepper in a shallow dish and mix well. Roll the chicken in the crumb mixture. Heat the butter in a nonstick skillet over medium-high heat. Add the chicken.

Cook for 5 minutes or until golden brown, turning occasionally. Add the mushrooms, onion, wine, bouillon cube and water. Bring to a boil; reduce heat to low. Simmer, covered, for 10 minutes, stirring occasionally. Add the grapes. Simmer for 5 minutes longer or until the chicken is cooked through, stirring occasionally. Spoon over the rice on a serving platter.

YIELD: 4 SERVINGS

CHICKEN BREASTS WITH ARTICHOKE HEARTS

6 boneless skinless chicken breasts
1 1/2 cups reduced-fat Italian salad dressing
1 (14-ounce) can artichoke hearts, drained
2 medium tomatoes, coarsely chopped
1 (6-ounce) can sliced mushrooms, drained
1/2 envelope onion soup mix
1/2 cup white wine
3 cups cooked brown rice

Arrange the chicken in a single layer in a 9x13-inch baking dish. Pour 1 cup of the Italian salad dressing over the chicken and turn to coat. Marinate, covered, in the refrigerator for 2 hours or longer, turning occasionally.

Layer the artichoke hearts, tomatoes and mushrooms over the chicken. Sprinkle with the onion soup mix. Drizzle with the remaining 1/2 cup Italian salad dressing and wine. Bake at 350 degrees for 1 hour or until the chicken is cooked through. Spoon over the brown rice on 6 dinner plates.

YIELD: 6 SERVINGS

R Facts ABOUT CALCIUM NEEDS OF CHILDREN

Check nutrition labels and talk to your child's pediatrician to assure that your child is receiving adequate amounts of calcium. Children require calcium to build strong bones and teeth.

UN-FRIED CHICKEN

12 chicken breasts, skinned
5 cups ice water
1 cup flour
1 cup seasoned bread crumbs
1 tablespoon Old Bay seasoning
$1/2$ teaspoon thyme
$1/2$ teaspoon oregano
$1/2$ teaspoon garlic powder
$1/2$ teaspoon Creole seasoning
$1/2$ teaspoon basil
$1/8$ teaspoon freshly ground black pepper
$1/8$ teaspoon cayenne pepper
$1^1/3$ cups plain nonfat yogurt

Combine the chicken and ice water in a large bowl. Let stand for 5 to 10 minutes. Combine the flour, bread crumbs, Old Bay seasoning, thyme, oregano, garlic powder, Creole seasoning, basil, black pepper and cayenne pepper in a sealable plastic bag; seal tightly. Shake to mix. Spoon the yogurt into a shallow dish.

Remove 2 pieces of the chicken from the ice water. Coat with the yogurt and then the flour mixture. Arrange the chicken on a baking sheet sprayed heavily with nonstick cooking spray. Repeat the process with the remaining chicken, yogurt and flour mixture.

Spray the chicken lightly with nonstick cooking spray. Arrange the baking sheet on the bottom oven rack. Bake at 400 degrees for 1 hour or until the chicken is cooked through, turning every 15 minutes.

YIELD: 12 SERVINGS

Sesame-Crusted Chicken with Orange Sauce

Chicken

2/3 cup dry seasoned bread crumbs
2/3 cup freshly grated Parmesan cheese
2/3 cup sesame seeds, toasted
6 boneless skinless chicken breasts
1/4 cup (1/2 stick) butter or margarine, melted

Orange Sauce

1 (10-ounce) jar currant jelly
3 tablespoons sherry
1/2 teaspoon Tabasco sauce
1/2 teaspoon ginger
1 (6-ounce) can frozen orange juice concentrate, thawed

To prepare the chicken, combine the bread crumbs, cheese and sesame seeds in a sealable plastic bag and shake to mix. Coat the chicken with the butter and then the crumb mixture. Arrange in a single layer in a shallow baking dish. Bake at 350 degrees for 1 hour or until the chicken is cooked through.

To prepare the sauce, combine the jelly, sherry, Tabasco sauce and ginger in a saucepan and mix well. Add the orange juice concentrate gradually, stirring constantly. Bring to a boil over medium heat, stirring frequently. Serve with the chicken.

Yield: 6 servings

THAI PEANUT CHICKEN AND VEGETABLES

LIGHTEN UP

Substitute reduced-sodium soy sauce for the soy sauce and reduced-fat peanut butter for the peanut butter.

1 pound boneless skinless chicken breasts
4 tablespoons soy sauce
1 garlic clove, finely chopped
1/4 teaspoon red pepper flakes
1/4 cup peanut butter
3 tablespoons vegetable oil
1 tablespoon brown sugar
1 large onion, thinly sliced
1/2 green bell pepper, julienned
1/2 red bell pepper, julienned
1/4 head red cabbage, shredded
2 cups cooked white rice

Cut the chicken into bite-size pieces. Whisk 3 tablespoons of the soy sauce, garlic and red pepper flakes in a large bowl. Add the chicken and toss to coat. Marinate at room temperature for 15 minutes, stirring twice. Combine the remaining 1 tablespoon soy sauce, peanut butter, 1 tablespoon of the oil and brown sugar in a medium bowl and mix until of a sauce consistency.

Stir-fry the chicken in the remaining 2 tablespoons oil in a skillet for 4 minutes. Add the onion and bell peppers. Stir-fry until the vegetables are tender-crisp. Add the cabbage and peanut sauce and mix well. Simmer, covered, for 2 minutes or until the cabbage is tender-crisp, stirring occasionally. Spoon over the rice on a serving platter.

YIELD: 4 SERVINGS

Spa Cuisine Lasagna

8 ounces lasagna noodles
1 pound ground turkey
1 cup finely chopped onion
2 garlic cloves, minced
1 (16-ounce) can chopped reduced-sodium tomatoes
1 (8-ounce) can tomato sauce
1 (6-ounce) can tomato paste
2 teaspoons basil
1 teaspoon oregano
1 teaspoon fennel seeds
1/8 teaspoon red pepper flakes
1 egg, beaten
3/4 cup freshly grated Parmesan cheese
2 cups reduced-fat cottage cheese
1 tablespoon parsley flakes
1/2 teaspoon black pepper
8 ounces part-skim mozzarella cheese, sliced

Cook the noodles using package directions, omitting the salt and fat; drain. Brown the ground turkey with the onion and garlic in a large saucepan, stirring until the ground turkey is crumbly; drain. Stir in the undrained tomatoes, tomato sauce, tomato paste, basil, oregano, fennel seeds and red pepper flakes. Simmer, covered, for 15 minutes, stirring frequently.

Combine the egg, half the Parmesan cheese, cottage cheese, parsley flakes and black pepper in a bowl and mix well. Layer the noodles, cottage cheese mixture, mozzarella cheese and ground turkey mixture in the order listed 1/2 at a time in a 9x13-inch baking pan sprayed with nonstick cooking spray. Sprinkle with the remaining Parmesan cheese. Bake at 375 degrees for 30 to 35 minutes or until bubbly. Let stand for 10 minutes before serving.

Yield: 8 servings

CORNISH HENS IN TARRAGON SAUCE

4 (^{3}/4-pound) Rock Cornish game hens
^{1}/2 teaspoon (or less) salt
^{1}/2 teaspoon freshly ground pepper
1^1/4 teaspoons tarragon
2 tablespoons butter or margarine
3 tablespoons finely chopped shallots
^{1}/3 cup dry white wine
^{1}/2 cup half-and-half
1 tablespoon finely chopped fresh parsley

Rub the game hens inside and outside with the salt and pepper. Place ^{1}/4 teaspoon of the tarragon in each cavity; truss. Heat the butter in an ovenproof baking pan until melted. Arrange the hens breast side up in the prepared pan and brush with the butter. Place the hens in the oven when the butter starts to sizzle. Bake at 450 degrees for 15 minutes; baste with the pan juices. Bake for 20 minutes longer or until the hens are tender, basting occasionally. Remove the hens to a serving platter with a slotted spoon, reserving the pan juices. Cover the hens to keep warm.

Skim the fat from the reserved pan juices. Stir the shallots into the reserved pan juices. Cook until tender, stirring constantly. Add the wine and stir to deglaze the pan. Add any accumulated juices from the hens and mix well. Simmer until the liquid is reduced by half, stirring constantly. Stir in the half-and-half and remaining ^{1}/4 teaspoon tarragon. Simmer just until heated through, stirring constantly. Strain the sauce and drizzle over the hens. Sprinkle with the parsley.

YIELD: 4 SERVINGS

BALSAMIC-GLAZED SALMON

4 teaspoons minced garlic
2 tablespoons olive oil
1/3 cup balsamic vinegar
4 teaspoons Dijon mustard
1 tablespoon honey
Salt and freshly ground pepper to taste
6 (6-ounce) salmon fillets
6 tablespoons julienned fresh basil leaves

Sauté the garlic in 1 tablespoon of the olive oil in a saucepan over medium heat for 3 minutes. Stir in the remaining 1 tablespoon olive oil, balsamic vinegar, Dijon mustard, honey, salt and pepper. Simmer for 3 minutes or until slightly thickened and of a glaze consistency, stirring constantly. Remove from heat. Cover to keep warm.

Arrange the salmon in a single layer in a foil-lined baking pan. Brush with some of the warm glaze. Bake at 475 degrees for 10 to 14 minutes or until the salmon flakes easily. Remove the salmon to a heated platter. Cover to keep warm.

Bring the remaining glaze to a boil, stirring occasionally. Boil for 1 to 2 minutes. Brush the salmon with the glaze. Sprinkle with the basil. Serve immediately.

YIELD: 6 SERVINGS

SALMON WITH BASIL VINAIGRETTE

RECIPE FOR BASIL VINAIGRETTE

Process 1/2 cup red wine vinegar, 1/2 cup balsamic vinegar, 1/2 cup packed chopped fresh basil, 2 teaspoons Asian red chile paste with garlic and 1 tablespoon minced garlic in a blender until smooth. Add 1/2 cup olive oil gradually, processing constantly until blended. Use immediately or store, covered, in the refrigerator for up to 2 days.

BASIL VINAIGRETTE (in sidebar)

CORN RELISH

3 cups frozen whole kernel corn, thawed, drained
1/2 cup chopped red bell pepper
1/2 cup chopped green bell pepper
1/2 cup chopped yellow bell pepper
1/2 cup chopped black olives
1/2 cup chopped red onion
Salt and pepper to taste

SALMON

4 (6-ounce) salmon fillets

ASSEMBLY

8 cups mixed baby greens
2 large tomatoes, thickly sliced

To prepare the relish, combine the corn, bell peppers, olives and onion in a bowl and mix well. Add 1/3 cup of the vinaigrette and toss to coat. Season with salt and pepper. Chill, covered, in the refrigerator for up to 4 hours.

To prepare the salmon, arrange the fillets in a single layer in a 9x13-inch baking dish. Drizzle with 3/4 cup of the vinaigrette, turning to coat. Marinate, covered, in the refrigerator for 1 to 8 hours, turning every 15 minutes; drain.

Arrange the fillets on a grill rack sprayed with nonstick cooking spray. Grill over hot coals for 8 to 10 minutes or until the salmon flakes easily, turning every 4 minutes. Remove to a heated platter. Cover to keep warm.

To assemble, toss the baby greens with the remaining vinaigrette in a bowl. Arrange the greens on 4 dinner plates. Spoon equal amounts of the corn relish on 1 side of each plate and arrange the sliced tomatoes next to the relish. Top with the salmon. Serve immediately.

YIELD: 4 SERVINGS

LIME SOY SWORDFISH

6 (6-ounce) swordfish steaks
2 tablespoons minced green onions
2 tablespoons fresh lime juice
1 1/2 tablespoons soy sauce
1 tablespoon corn oil
1 1/2 teaspoons Dijon mustard
1 teaspoon grated lime zest
1 garlic clove, minced
1/4 teaspoon freshly ground white pepper

Arrange the steaks in a single layer in a shallow dish. Combine the green onions, lime juice, soy sauce, corn oil, Dijon mustard, zest, garlic and white pepper in a bowl and mix well. Pour over the steaks and turn to coat. Marinate, covered, in the refrigerator for 2 to 4 hours, turning occasionally.

Place the swordfish on a grill rack sprayed with nonstick cooking spray. Grill over medium-hot coals for 4 to 5 minutes per side or until the swordfish flakes easily, turning once. Remove to a serving platter. Garnish with additional minced green onions. You may broil in the oven if a grill is not available.

YIELD: 6 SERVINGS

PACIFIC GRILLED TUNA

6 (6-ounce) tuna steaks, $^3/_4$ inch thick
1 cup thinly sliced green onions
$^1/_4$ cup plus 2 tablespoons reduced-sodium soy sauce
$^1/_4$ cup plus 2 tablespoons rice wine vinegar
1 tablespoon sesame oil
1 tablespoon grated gingerroot
$^1/_4$ teaspoon red pepper flakes

Arrange the tuna in a single layer in a shallow dish. Combine the green onions, soy sauce, wine vinegar, sesame oil, gingerroot and red pepper flakes in a bowl and mix well. Reserve $^1/_4$ of the marinade mixture.

Pour the remaining marinade over the tuna, turning to coat. Marinate, covered, in the refrigerator for 2 hours or longer, turning occasionally; drain.

Place the tuna on a grill rack sprayed with nonstick cooking spray. Grill over medium-hot coals for 4 minutes per side or until the tuna flakes easily, basting frequently with the reserved marinade.

YIELD: 6 SERVINGS

CRAB MANICOTTI

16 large manicotti shells
2 cups reduced-fat ricotta cheese
1 (6-ounce) can crab meat, drained, flaked
$^3/_4$ cup shredded part-skim mozzarella cheese
1 teaspoon parsley flakes
3 garlic cloves, minced
$^1/_2$ teaspoon seasoned salt
$^1/_2$ teaspoon lemon pepper
1 small onion
1 zucchini, chopped
1 green bell pepper, chopped
1 (16-ounce) can diced tomatoes
1 (6-ounce) can tomato paste
Sugar to taste
Italian seasoning to taste
$^1/_4$ cup freshly grated Parmesan cheese

LIGHTEN UP

Substitute nonfat cottage cheese for the ricotta cheese and no-added-salt diced tomatoes for the diced tomatoes.

Cook the pasta using package directions, omitting the salt and fat; drain. Rinse and drain. Combine the ricotta cheese, crab meat, $^1/_4$ cup of the mozzarella cheese, parsley flakes, 1 of the garlic cloves, seasoned salt and lemon pepper in a bowl and mix well.

Sauté the onion, zucchini and bell pepper in a nonstick skillet sprayed with nonstick cooking spray until the vegetables are tender. Stir in the undrained tomatoes, tomato paste, remaining 2 garlic cloves, sugar and Italian seasoning. Simmer until the sauce is slightly thickened, stirring occasionally.

Stuff the pasta shells with the ricotta cheese mixture. Arrange the shells in a single layer in a baking pan. Spoon the tomato sauce over the top. Sprinkle with the Parmesan cheese and the remaining $^1/_2$ cup mozzarella cheese. Bake at 350 degrees for 30 minutes or until bubbly.

YIELD: 8 SERVINGS

SCALLOPS À LA PROVENÇAL

3 garlic cloves, minced
3 tablespoons olive oil
1 medium onion, thinly sliced
2 tablespoons chopped fresh Italian parsley
2 tablespoons chopped fresh basil
1 (14-ounce) can artichoke hearts, drained, cut into quarters
1 pound fresh sea scallops
12 ounces medium shrimp, peeled, deveined
1 pound fresh mushrooms, sliced
1 tomato, chopped
1 (6-ounce) can pitted black olives, drained, sliced
Juice of 1 lemon
Salt and pepper to taste
3/4 to 1 cup half-and-half
12 ounces angel hair pasta, cooked, drained

Sauté the garlic in the olive oil in a skillet. Add the onion, parsley and basil. Sauté until the onion is tender. Stir in the artichokes. Cook for 5 minutes, stirring frequently. Add the scallops and shrimp and mix well.

Simmer, covered, for 10 minutes, stirring occasionally. Add the mushrooms, tomato, olives and lemon juice and mix well. Simmer for 5 minutes, stirring frequently. Season with salt and pepper. Add just enough of the half-and-half to make of a sauce consistency and mix well. Simmer for 10 minutes longer, stirring frequently. Spoon over the hot pasta on a serving platter.

YIELD: 6 SERVINGS

ROASTED RED PEPPER AND SCALLOP FETTUCCINI

2 red bell peppers
1 teaspoon vegetable oil
16 ounces fettuccini
1/4 cup (1/2 stick) butter or margarine
1/2 cup finely chopped green onions
2 teaspoons finely chopped garlic
1 1/2 pounds large scallops
2 cups sour cream
Salt and freshly ground white pepper to taste

Rub the bell peppers with the oil. Arrange on a baking sheet. Roast at 400 degrees for 25 minutes or until the skins are blistered and charred on all sides, turning frequently. Place the bell peppers in a sealable plastic bag immediately and seal tightly. Allow to steam in the bag until cool. Peel, seed and coarsely chop the cooled bell peppers.

Process the bell peppers in a blender at high speed until smooth. Cook the pasta using package directions, omitting the salt and fat; drain. Cover to keep warm. Heat the butter in a skillet over medium heat until melted. Add the green onions and garlic. Cook until the green onions are tender, stirring frequently. Add the scallops.

Cook for 5 to 7 minutes or until the scallops are tender, stirring frequently. Stir in the red pepper purée and sour cream. Cook for 4 to 6 minutes longer or until heated through, stirring occasionally; do not boil. Combine with the pasta in a large bowl and toss to mix. Season with salt and white pepper. Serve immediately.

YIELD: 8 SERVINGS

LIGHTEN UP

Substitute nonfat sour cream or nonfat yogurt for the sour cream.

Scallops Florentine

2 bunches fresh spinach, trimmed
2 tablespoons fresh orange juice
1 teaspoon Dijon mustard
Freshly ground pepper to taste
4 tablespoons olive oil
2 tablespoons chopped fresh chives
Salt to taste
1 1/2 pounds sea scallops
2 teaspoons finely grated orange zest

Rinse the spinach; do not shake off the excess water. Cook the spinach in a saucepan over medium heat for 3 minutes, stirring once; drain. Cover to keep warm. Whisk the orange juice, Dijon mustard and pepper in a bowl. Add 2 tablespoons of the olive oil gradually, whisking constantly until blended. Stir in 1 tablespoon of the chives and salt.

Cook the scallops 1/2 at a time in the remaining 2 tablespoons olive oil in a large nonstick skillet until opaque and golden brown on the edges, turning once. Spoon the spinach onto a serving platter. Arrange the scallops over the spinach. Drizzle with the orange juice mixture. Sprinkle with the remaining 1 tablespoon chives and zest.

Yield: 6 servings

Fettuccini with Crab and Shrimp Florentine

6 ounces fettuccini
1 (10-ounce) package frozen chopped spinach, thawed, drained
4 ounces fresh mushrooms, sliced
1 small onion, finely chopped
1 garlic clove, finely chopped
4 tablespoons olive oil
1 cup flaked crab meat
1 teaspoon basil
Salt and pepper to taste
1^1/$_2$ pounds shrimp, steamed, peeled, deveined
8 ounces mozzarella cheese, shredded
^{1}/$_4$ cup freshly grated Parmesan cheese

Cook the pasta using package directions until al dente, omitting the salt and fat; drain. Cover to keep warm. Press the excess moisture from the spinach.

Sauté the mushrooms, onion and garlic in 2 tablespoons of the olive oil in a skillet until the onion is tender. Stir in the spinach. Cook until heated through, stirring constantly. Add the crab meat, basil, salt and pepper and mix gently.

Line an oiled 7x11-inch baking dish with the pasta. Layer the shrimp and the spinach mixture over the pasta. Sprinkle with the mozzarella cheese. Drizzle with the remaining 2 tablespoons olive oil. Bake at 375 degrees until bubbly. Sprinkle with the Parmesan cheese.

Yield: 6 servings

Lighten Up

Decrease the olive oil to 2 tablespoons, sautéing the mushrooms, onion and garlic in a nonstick skillet sprayed heavily with nonstick olive oil cooking spray. Drizzle the 2 tablespoons olive oil over the prepared layers. Substitute part-skim mozzarella cheese for the mozzarella cheese.

MEDITERRANEAN SHRIMP PASTA

16 ounces linguini
1 pound medium shrimp, peeled, deveined
1 teaspoon minced garlic
Seasoned salt and freshly ground pepper to taste
1/4 cup olive oil
1/2 cup chopped sun-dried tomatoes
1/3 cup pine nuts
Juice of 1 lemon

Cook the pasta using package directions, omitting the salt and fat; drain. Sauté the shrimp, garlic, seasoned salt and pepper in the olive oil for 5 minutes. Add the sun-dried tomatoes and pine nuts and mix well.

Sauté for 1 minute or until the shrimp turn pink. Toss the shrimp mixture with the pasta in a bowl until mixed. Drizzle with the lemon juice.

YIELD: 6 SERVINGS

BROCCOLI BLEU CHEESE LINGUINI

12 ounces linguini
1 bunch broccoli
4 garlic cloves, chopped
2 scallions, finely chopped
1/2 cup (1 stick) butter or margarine
3/4 cup whipping cream
Salt and freshly ground pepper to taste
4 ounces bleu cheese, crumbled
1/4 cup freshly grated Parmesan cheese

Cook the pasta using package directions, omitting the salt and fat; drain. Cover to keep warm. Discard only the coarse part of the broccoli stems. Sliver the remaining stems and separate the florets into bite-size pieces. Steam the broccoli just until tender-crisp; drain.

Sauté the broccoli, garlic and scallions in the butter in a skillet for 3 minutes. Stir in the whipping cream, salt and pepper. Simmer for 5 to 10 minutes or until slightly thickened, stirring constantly. Combine the broccoli mixture and pasta in a bowl and mix gently. Add the bleu cheese and toss to mix. Add the Parmesan cheese and mix well.

YIELD: 6 SERVINGS

FETTUCCINI WITH TWO-OLIVE SAUCE

12 ounces fettuccini
2 garlic cloves, minced
$1/4$ cup olive oil
1 (6-ounce) can pitted black olives, drained, chopped
1 (3-ounce) jar pimento-stuffed green olives, drained, chopped
$1/2$ cup water
1 small bunch parsley, finely chopped
1 teaspoon oregano
$1/2$ teaspoon red pepper flakes
$3/4$ cup freshly grated Parmesan cheese

Cook the pasta using package directions, omitting the salt and fat; drain. Cover to keep warm. Sauté the garlic in the olive oil in a skillet over medium-high heat just until the garlic begins to turn brown. Stir in the next 6 ingredients. Bring just to a boil over high heat, stirring occasionally. Spoon over the hot pasta on a serving platter. Sprinkle with the cheese.

YIELD: 6 SERVINGS

BRIE AND TOMATO PASTA

4 pounds fresh tomatoes, chopped
$3/4$ cup chopped sun-dried tomatoes
$1/2$ cup olive oil
$1/2$ bunch spinach, trimmed, torn into bite-size pieces
8 ounces Brie cheese, chopped
2 tablespoons each minced garlic and chopped fresh basil
1 tablespoon chopped fresh parsley
1 teaspoon freshly ground pepper
16 ounces linguini
$1/3$ cup freshly grated Parmesan cheese

Combine all the ingredients except the linguini and Parmesan cheese in a bowl and mix gently. Let stand, covered, at room temperature for 4 to 12 hours, stirring occasionally. Cook the pasta using package directions, omitting the salt and fat; drain. Add the tomato mixture and toss to mix. Spoon into a pasta bowl. Sprinkle with the Parmesan cheese.

YIELD: 8 SERVINGS

PENNE WITH BLACK BEANS AND ARTICHOKE HEARTS

1 cup sliced green onions
1 tablespoon olive oil
2 (14-ounce) cans diced tomatoes
1 garlic clove, minced
3/4 teaspoon oregano
1/4 teaspoon salt
1/8 teaspoon red pepper flakes
1/8 teaspoon black pepper
1 (16-ounce) can black beans, drained, rinsed
4 cups hot cooked penne
1 (14-ounce) can artichoke hearts, drained, cut into quarters

Sauté the green onions in the olive oil in a nonstick skillet over medium heat until tender. Stir in the undrained tomatoes, garlic, oregano, salt, red pepper flakes and black pepper. Simmer, covered, for 10 minutes, stirring occasionally. Add the beans and mix well.

Simmer, covered, for 5 minutes longer, stirring occasionally. Combine the bean mixture, pasta and artichoke hearts in a bowl and toss gently.

YIELD: 6 SERVINGS

GREEK-STYLE PASTA WITH MINT

16 ounces penne
1 1/3 cups crumbled feta cheese
1 (6-ounce) can pitted black olives, drained, sliced
1/4 cup chopped fresh mint
2 tablespoons olive oil
Juice of 1 lemon
1/8 teaspoon pepper
1 cup torn arugula

Cook the pasta using package directions, omitting the salt and fat; drain. Cover to keep warm. Combine the feta cheese, olives, mint, olive oil, lemon juice and pepper in a bowl and mix well. Add the pasta and arugula and toss to mix. Serve immediately.

YIELD: 8 SERVINGS

ITALIAN VEGETABLE LASAGNA

1 onion, finely chopped
3 garlic cloves, minced
2 tablespoons vegetable oil
2 pounds fresh mushrooms, sliced
$1/4$ teaspoon red pepper flakes
2 pounds fresh spinach, torn into bite-size pieces
2 cups ricotta cheese
1 cup freshly grated Parmesan cheese
3 tablespoons chopped fresh basil
$1/4$ teaspoon black pepper
8 ounces uncooked lasagna noodles
4 cups shredded mozzarella cheese
$1^1/4$ cups shredded sharp Cheddar cheese
1 (4-ounce) jar roasted red peppers, drained, julienned

Sauté the onion and garlic in the oil in a nonstick skillet until the onion is tender. Add the mushrooms and red pepper flakes and mix well. Cook over medium-high heat just until the mushrooms are tender. Stir in the spinach. Cook until the spinach wilts, stirring occasionally.

Combine the ricotta cheese, Parmesan cheese, basil and black pepper in a bowl and mix well. Spread $1/3$ of the spinach mixture in a 9x13-inch baking pan. Layer with half the lasagna noodles and $1/2$ of the remaining spinach mixture. Spread with the ricotta cheese mixture. Sprinkle with half the mozzarella cheese, half the Cheddar cheese and the roasted red peppers. Cover with the remaining lasagna noodles, overlapping if necessary. Top with the remaining spinach mixture and any liquid in the skillet.

Place the baking pan on a baking sheet. Bake at 350 degrees for 15 minutes. Sprinkle with the remaining mozzarella cheese and remaining Cheddar cheese. Bake for 15 to 20 minutes longer or until brown and bubbly. Let stand for 15 minutes before serving.

YIELD: 8 SERVINGS

Rx FACTS ABOUT HEALTHY LIVING

Incorporating the following into your lifestyle will help reduce the risk of many diseases including heart disease, stroke, diabetes, and cancer:

❋ *Don't smoke.*

❋ *Have your blood pressure and blood sugar checked at least once a year (ask your pharmacist if he/she can do this for you).*

❋ *Eat foods that are lower in fat, salt, and cholesterol.*

❋ *Exercise regularly and stay active.*

❋ *Maintain your ideal weight.*

❋ *Avoid drinking excessive amounts of alcohol.*

Green Beans in Basil Sauce

5 sprigs of parsley
1 bay leaf
$^1/_2$ stalk celery
2 sprigs of thyme
1$^1/_2$ pounds fresh green beans, trimmed
2 medium onions, thinly sliced
5 tablespoons olive oil
4 medium tomatoes, chopped
Salt and freshly ground pepper to taste
$^1/_2$ cup chopped fresh basil
2 garlic cloves
$^1/_4$ cup chopped fresh parsley

Tie the parsley sprigs, bay leaf, celery and thyme in cheesecloth to make a bouquet garni. Combine the green beans with enough water to cover in a saucepan. Bring to a boil; reduce heat. Cook for 5 minutes or until tender-crisp; drain. Plunge into ice water in a bowl; drain.

Sauté the onions in 3 tablespoons of the olive oil in a nonstick saucepan until tender. Stir in the tomatoes, salt and pepper. Add the bouquet garni. Cook over medium-high heat for 10 to 15 minutes or until thickened, stirring frequently. Remove the bouquet garni and discard. Stir in the green beans. Simmer, covered, for 5 minutes, stirring occasionally.

Process the remaining 2 tablespoons olive oil, basil, garlic and chopped parsley in a blender until puréed. Add to the bean mixture and mix well. Simmer just until heated through, stirring frequently. Serve hot or chilled.

Yield: 6 servings

CALIFORNIA EGGPLANT

3 medium unpeeled eggplant
8 ounces fresh mushrooms, chopped
1 cup chopped onion
2 garlic cloves, minced
Salt and pepper to taste
3 tablespoons butter or margarine
1 1/2 cups cottage cheese
1 cup cooked brown rice
1 cup shredded sharp Cheddar cheese
1/2 teaspoon thyme
1/8 teaspoon Tabasco sauce
1/4 cup sunflower kernels, toasted
Paprika to taste
1/2 cup chopped fresh parsley

*Cut the eggplant lengthwise into halves. Scoop out the centers, leaving
1/4-inch shells. Chop the centers.*

*Sauté the chopped eggplant, mushrooms, onion, garlic, salt and
pepper in the butter in a skillet until the vegetables are tender. Stir in the
cottage cheese, brown rice, Cheddar cheese, thyme, Tabasco sauce and
sunflower kernels.*

*Spoon the eggplant mixture into the shells. Sprinkle with the
paprika and parsley. Arrange the shells in a greased baking pan. Bake at
350 degrees for 40 minutes or until brown and bubbly.*

YIELD: 6 SERVINGS

LIGHTEN UP

*Omit the butter and
sauté the vegetables
in a nonstick skillet
sprayed with nonstick
cooking spray.
Substitute nonfat
cottage cheese for
the cottage cheese.*

MICROWAVE VIDALIA ONIONS

4 medium Vidalia onions, peeled
4 ounces cream cheese, softened
1/4 cup whipping cream
1/4 cup shredded Cheddar cheese
2 slices crisp-cooked bacon, crumbled
1/4 cup sliced fresh mushrooms
1/4 cup finely chopped red bell pepper
1/4 cup chopped fresh chives
1/2 teaspoon salt
1/2 teaspoon garlic powder
1/4 teaspoon pepper
16 small shrimp, steamed, peeled, deveined
Paprika to taste

Wrap each onion in a damp paper towel. Microwave on High for 8 to 10 minutes or until tender. Remove the inside pulp of each onion carefully, leaving 3 layers of onion. Discard the pulp. Arrange the shells in a microwave-safe dish.

Beat the cream cheese, whipping cream and Cheddar cheese in a mixing bowl until blended. Stir in the bacon, mushrooms, bell pepper, chives, salt, garlic powder and pepper. Spoon into the onion shells.

Microwave on High for 2 to 3 minutes or until heated through. Arrange on a serving platter. Top each stuffed onion with 4 shrimp. Sprinkle with paprika. Serve immediately.

YIELD: 4 SERVINGS

LEMON BASIL SUGAR SNAPS

3 pounds sugar snap peas, trimmed
4 teaspoons olive oil
1 cup chopped fresh basil
2 teaspoons grated lemon zest
1 teaspoon white pepper
3/4 teaspoon salt

Sauté the peas in the olive oil in a large nonstick skillet for 3 minutes or until tender-crisp. Stir in the basil, zest, white pepper and salt. Sauté for 1 minute longer. Spoon into a serving bowl. Serve immediately.

YIELD: 8 SERVINGS ▬▬▬

NEW POTATOES WITH PROSCIUTTO

6 large red new potatoes, cut into wedges
1 green bell pepper, chopped
1 large onion, chopped
6 slices prosciutto, cut into bite-size pieces
2 tablespoons olive oil
1 teaspoon salt
Garlic powder to taste
Pepper to taste
Rosemary to taste
Thyme to taste

Combine the new potatoes, bell pepper, onion and prosciutto in a baking pan and toss gently. Drizzle with the olive oil. Sprinkle with the salt, garlic powder, pepper, rosemary and thyme.

Roast at 400 degrees for 45 minutes or until the onion and potatoes are tender, stirring occasionally. Serve with your favorite grilled entrée.

YIELD: 6 SERVINGS ▬▬▬

R𝗑 FACTS ABOUT ANTIOXIDANTS

Tomatoes (raw, cooked, or tomato products such as sauces or ketchup), grapefruit, and watermelon are rich in lycopenes. These vitamin-like substances are antioxidants that help prevent damage to DNA and may help lower prostate cancer risk.

MOROCCAN NEW POTATOES

2 pounds medium new potatoes, cut into quarters
1 1/2 tablespoons olive oil
1 tablespoon butter or margarine
1/4 cup fresh lime juice
2 large garlic cloves, finely chopped
2 teaspoons coriander seeds, crushed
1 bunch green onions with tops, minced
1/2 to 3/4 cup chopped fresh cilantro
1 1/2 teaspoons chili powder
Salt and pepper to taste
1/4 cup freshly grated Parmesan cheese

Combine the potatoes with enough water to cover in a saucepan. Bring to a boil. Boil just until tender; drain. Heat the olive oil, butter, lime juice, garlic and coriander seeds in a saucepan until the butter melts, stirring frequently. Toss with the potatoes in a serving bowl.

Add the green onions, cilantro, chili powder, salt and pepper to the potato mixture and toss to coat. Sprinkle with the cheese. Serve warm or at room temperature. These potatoes are just as good the following day.

YIELD: 10 SERVINGS

WILD MUSHROOM AND ASPARAGUS RISOTTO

12 medium asparagus spears, trimmed, cut into 1-inch pieces
6 ounces bacon, chopped
2 medium onions, finely chopped
12 ounces fresh morels or other wild mushrooms
$^1/_4$ cup ($^1/_2$ stick) butter or margarine
$1^1/_2$ cups arborio rice
3 to 4 cups chicken stock
$^2/_3$ cup freshly grated Parmesan cheese
Salt and freshly ground pepper to taste

Steam the asparagus until tender-crisp; drain. Fry the bacon in a large saucepan until light brown. Add the onions and mix well. Cook until the onions are tender, stirring constantly. Cook the morels in the butter in a skillet until tender, stirring frequently. Stir into the onion mixture. Add the rice and mix well.

　　Heat the chicken stock in a saucepan just to the simmering point. Stir $^1/_2$ cup of the hot stock into the rice mixture in the large saucepan. Cook until most of the liquid has been absorbed, stirring constantly. Add the remaining chicken stock $^1/_2$ cup at a time. Cook until the stock is absorbed after each addition. Continue cooking until the rice is tender and the mixture is creamy and thick. Stir in the asparagus, cheese, salt and pepper. Serve immediately.

YIELD: 8 SERVINGS

LIGHTEN UP

Substitute Canadian bacon for the cured bacon. Omit the butter and use margarine to decrease the cholesterol and substitute reduced-sodium chicken broth for the chicken stock to reduce the sodium.

PERSIAN RICE PILAF

1 cup white wine
1 cup water
$^1/_3$ cup chopped green bell pepper
$^1/_3$ cup chopped red bell pepper
$^1/_4$ cup minced onion
1 chicken bouillon cube
Salt and freshly ground pepper to taste
1 cup white rice
$^1/_4$ cup ($^1/_2$ stick) butter or margarine
$^1/_2$ cup golden raisins
$^1/_3$ cup chopped black olives
$^1/_3$ cup slivered almonds
$^1/_2$ teaspoon grated lemon zest
$^1/_2$ teaspoon curry powder
$^1/_4$ cup chopped fresh parsley

Combine the white wine, water, bell peppers, onion, bouillon cube, salt and pepper in a saucepan and mix well. Bring to a boil. Stir in the rice; reduce heat. Simmer, covered, for 20 minutes or until the rice is tender and the liquid has been absorbed.

Heat the butter in a saucepan over medium-low heat until melted. Stir in the golden raisins. Cook for 3 to 4 minutes or until heated through, stirring frequently. Stir in the olives, almonds and zest. Remove from heat. Stir the raisin mixture and curry powder into the rice mixture. Spoon into a serving bowl. Sprinkle with the parsley.

YIELD: 4 SERVINGS

SPAGHETTI SQUASH CARBONARA

1 (3-pound) spaghetti squash
4 ounces smoked ham, julienned
1/4 cup chopped green onions
1 garlic clove, minced
3 tablespoons vegetable oil
1 cup snow peas, julienned
1/4 cup chopped red bell pepper
3 eggs
1/4 cup freshly grated Parmesan cheese
Freshly ground pepper

Cut the squash lengthwise into halves. Scoop out the seeds. Arrange the squash cut side down in a 9x13-inch baking pan. Add enough water to the baking pan to measure 1/2 inch. Bake at 350 degrees for 35 to 40 minutes or until the squash is tender.

Sauté the ham, green onions and garlic in the oil in a skillet until the green onions are tender. Stir in the snow peas and bell pepper. Sauté for 2 minutes. Remove from heat.

Whisk the eggs and cheese in a bowl until mixed. Turn the cooked squash halves cut side up. Pull out the strands of the squash with a fork, working carefully so as not to tear the squash shells. Add the hot squash strands to the egg mixture and toss to mix. Stir in the ham mixture. Spoon the squash mixture into the shells. Sprinkle with pepper. Arrange the shells on a baking sheet. Bake at 350 degrees just until heated through. Serve immediately.

YIELD: 2 SERVINGS

LIGHTEN UP

Omit the oil and sauté the ham, green onions and garlic in a nonstick skillet sprayed heavily with nonstick cooking spray. Substitute 6 egg whites for the whole eggs or the equivalent amount of egg substitute.

TWICE-BAKED SWEET POTATOES

LIGHTEN UP

Omit the corn oil and spray the sweet potatoes with nonstick cooking spray. Substitute reduced-fat cream cheese for the cream cheese. Decrease the pecans to 1/4 cup coarsely chopped toasted pecans.

12 small sweet potatoes
1 1/2 tablespoons corn oil
8 ounces cream cheese, softened
1/4 cup packed brown sugar
1/4 cup (1/2 stick) butter or margarine, softened
2 tablespoons sherry
1 1/4 teaspoons salt
1/2 teaspoon pepper
1/2 cup coarsely chopped pecans

Prick the sweet potatoes with a fork. Rub lightly with the corn oil. Arrange on a baking sheet. Bake at 375 degrees for 1 hour or until tender; reduce the oven temperature to 350 degrees. Cool the sweet potatoes slightly. Cut a thin strip from the top of each. Scoop out the pulp carefully, leaving the shells intact.

Beat the sweet potato pulp in a mixing bowl until smooth. Add the cream cheese, brown sugar, butter, sherry, salt and pepper. Beat until blended, scraping the bowl occasionally. Spoon the sweet potato mixture into the shells. Sprinkle with the pecans. You may prepare to this stage up to 2 days in advance and store, covered, in the refrigerator.

Arrange the stuffed sweet potatoes on a baking sheet sprayed with nonstick cooking spray. Bake for 30 minutes or until heated through.

YIELD: 12 SERVINGS

Summer Tomato Basil Tart

Pastry

2 cups flour
2 tablespoons sugar
4 teaspoons baking powder
$1/4$ teaspoon salt
$1/3$ cup shortening
$3/4$ cup buttermilk

Tomato Filling

6 medium tomatoes, chopped
2 teaspoons chopped fresh basil
$1/2$ teaspoon salt
1 cup mayonnaise
1 cup shredded Cheddar cheese
1 cup shredded Swiss cheese
2 tablespoons freshly grated Parmesan cheese

To prepare the pastry, combine the flour, sugar, baking powder and salt in a bowl and mix well. Cut in the shortening until crumbly. Add the buttermilk and stir just until moistened. Let the pastry rest for 30 minutes. Press over the bottom of a 9-inch springform pan. Bake at 450 degrees for 10 minutes or until light brown.

To prepare the filling, combine the tomatoes, basil and salt in a bowl and mix gently. Spoon over the baked pastry. Combine the mayonnaise, Cheddar cheese, Swiss cheese and Parmesan cheese in a bowl and mix well. Spread over the tomato mixture. Bake at 400 degrees for 15 minutes or until brown and bubbly.

Yield: 8 servings

YELLOW PEPPERS WITH CURRANTS AND SUN-DRIED TOMATOES

1 cup white rice
1/4 cup currants
1/3 cup orange juice
2 small yellow onions, finely chopped
2 garlic cloves, minced
2 tablespoons olive oil
1 tablespoon chopped sun-dried tomatoes
1 tablespoon chopped fresh basil
1 tablespoon chopped fresh parsley
1 teaspoon coriander
Salt and pepper to taste
4 large yellow bell peppers

Cook the rice using package directions, omitting the salt and fat. Plump the currants in the orange juice in a bowl; drain.

Cook the yellow onions and garlic in the olive oil in a skillet over medium-low heat for 10 minutes, stirring frequently. Stir in the rice, currants, sun-dried tomatoes, basil, parsley, coriander, salt and pepper.

Cut the tops from the bell peppers, reserving the tops. Discard the seeds and membranes. Spoon the rice mixture into the bell peppers. Replace the tops. Arrange the stuffed bell peppers in an 8x8-baking dish coated with olive oil. Bake, covered, at 350 degrees for 30 to 35 minutes or until the bell peppers are tender; remove cover. Bake for 15 minutes longer or until light brown. Serve hot or at room temperature.

YIELD: 4 SERVINGS

Vegetable Tofu Stir-Fry with Almonds

2 teaspoons cornstarch
1 cup cold water
2 tablespoons soy sauce
2 teaspoons chicken bouillon granules
1 garlic clove, crushed
1 cup thinly sliced carrots
1 cup diagonally sliced fresh green beans
2 tablespoons vegetable oil
1 cup cauliflower florets, chopped
1 onion, thinly sliced
1 cup cubed firm tofu
$1/2$ cup almond slivers, toasted

Add the cornstarch to the cold water in a bowl, whisking until dissolved. Stir in the soy sauce, bouillon granules and garlic. Stir-fry the carrots and green beans in the oil in a skillet over medium-high heat for 2 minutes. Add the cauliflower and onion.

Stir-fry for 2 minutes. Add the soy sauce mixture and mix well. Cook until thickened, stirring constantly. Add the tofu and mix well. Stir-fry for 2 minutes. Spoon into a serving bowl. Sprinkle with the almonds. Serve with brown rice.

Yield: 4 servings

CONFETTI VEGETABLE FRITTERS

LIGHTEN UP

Omit the oil and bake the fritters on a baking sheet sprayed with nonstick cooking spray at 375 degrees until brown on both sides, turning once.

1 cup finely shredded carrots
1 cup finely shredded peeled baking potatoes
1 cup finely shredded zucchini
1 large onion, finely chopped
$1/4$ cup flour
2 eggs, beaten
$1/2$ teaspoon salt
$1/4$ to $1/2$ teaspoon poultry seasoning
$1/8$ teaspoon Worcestershire sauce
$1/8$ teaspoon cayenne pepper
2 tablespoons vegetable oil

Combine the carrots, potatoes, zucchini and onion in a bowl and mix well. Whisk the flour, eggs, salt, poultry seasoning, Worcestershire sauce and cayenne pepper in a bowl. Add to the carrot mixture and mix well.

Heat the oil in a large skillet until hot. Drop the batter by $1/4$ cupfuls into the hot oil in the skillet; flatten with a spatula. Fry the fritters for 4 to 5 minutes per side or until golden brown; drain. Serve with applesauce or sour cream.

YIELD: 8 FRITTERS

VEGETABLE AND POLENTA SQUARES

1 small red bell pepper, chopped
1 small yellow bell pepper, chopped
1 small onion, chopped
1 tablespoon olive oil
2 unpeeled medium zucchini, thinly sliced
1 garlic clove, minced
2 teaspoons basil
8 ounces mozzarella cheese, shredded
4 cups water
1 cup cornmeal
1 (17-ounce) can whole kernel corn, drained, rinsed
1 (16-ounce) can Italian-style crushed tomatoes, heated

Sauté the bell peppers and onion in the olive oil in a skillet for 5 minutes. Stir in the zucchini and garlic. Cook until the zucchini is tender, stirring constantly. Add the basil and mix well. Stir in the cheese. Remove from heat.

Bring the water to a boil in a saucepan over high heat; reduce heat to medium. Sprinkle the cornmeal over the boiling water. Cook over low heat until the polenta is thick and creamy, stirring constantly. Remove from heat. Stir in the corn.

Spread half the polenta in a greased 8x8-inch baking dish. Spread the zucchini mixture over the polenta using a slotted spoon. Top with the remaining polenta.

Let stand for 10 minutes. Bake at 400 degrees for 15 minutes or just until heated through. Cut into squares. Top each square with some of the warm tomatoes.

YIELD: 6 SERVINGS

R Facts
ABOUT
IMMUNIZATION

Do not forget to periodically update your immunization card. Talk with your pharmacist or doctor about which vaccines you may need. Some vaccines need to be updated more frequently than others (i.e. influenza).

CHEESY EGG CASSEROLE

1 cup flour
1 teaspoon baking powder
16 ounces Monterey Jack cheese, shredded
4 cups small curd reduced-fat cottage cheese
1 (4-ounce) can diced green chiles, drained
10 eggs, beaten
$1/2$ cup (1 stick) butter or margarine, melted

Combine the flour and baking powder in a bowl and mix well. Combine the Monterey Jack cheese, cottage cheese and chiles in a bowl and mix well. Stir in the flour mixture, beaten eggs and butter. Spoon into a greased 9x13-inch baking dish.

Bake at 400 degrees for 15 minutes. Reduce the oven temperature to 350 degrees. Bake for 30 minutes longer or until golden brown and set. For a spicier version, substitute Pepper Jack cheese for the Monterey Jack cheese.

YIELD: 10 SERVINGS

Huevos Rancheros Casserole

3/4 cup chopped onion
1/2 cup finely chopped Anaheim chile
1/2 jalapeño chile, minced
4 1/2 teaspoons vegetable oil
5 eggs
3 egg whites
1/3 cup milk
1 tablespoon taco sauce
3/4 teaspoon salt
5 (7-inch) corn tortillas, torn into bite-size pieces
1 medium tomato, chopped
1 cup shredded sharp Cheddar cheese
1 cup shredded Pepper Jack cheese
2 tablespoons coarsely chopped cilantro

Sauté the onion, Anaheim chile and jalapeño chile in 1 1/2 teaspoons of the oil in a skillet for 4 minutes. Whisk the eggs and egg whites in a large bowl until blended. Stir in the milk, taco sauce and salt. Add the corn tortillas and onion mixture and mix well.

Heat the remaining 3 teaspoons oil in a skillet until hot. Add the egg mixture. Scramble for 2 minutes or until partially cooked. Remove from heat. Stir in the tomato, 3/4 cup of the Cheddar cheese and 3/4 cup of the Pepper Jack cheese. Spoon into a 9x9-inch baking dish sprayed with nonstick cooking spray. Sprinkle with the remaining 1/4 cup Cheddar cheese and remaining 1/4 cup Pepper Jack Cheese.

Bake at 400 degrees for 25 minutes or until light brown. Sprinkle with the cilantro. Serve with pico de gallo, sliced avocado and/or sour cream.

Yield: 4 servings

Rx Facts about Arthritis

One in every seven Americans of all ages is afflicted with arthritis. There are more than 100 different types of arthritis, which usually affect the joints; some types may affect the muscles, connective tissue, heart, lungs, eyes, skin, and bone marrow. More information can be accessed on-line at the Arthritis Foundation at www.arthritis.org.

MUSHROOM AND SPINACH QUICHE

LIGHTEN UP

Replace the whole milk with skim milk. Sauté the mushrooms and onion in a nonstick skillet sprayed with nonstick cooking spray, thus omitting the 2 tablespoons butter. Substitute the whipping cream with half-and-half and reduce the Swiss cheese to 1 cup.

2 (10-ounce) packages frozen chopped spinach, thawed, drained
1 recipe (2-crust) pie pastry
8 ounces fresh mushrooms, chopped
$1/4$ cup chopped onion
2 tablespoons butter or margarine
$1^1/2$ cups whipping cream
6 eggs
1 cup milk
2 tablespoons flour
1 teaspoon salt
$1/8$ teaspoon nutmeg
$1/8$ teaspoon cayenne pepper
$1/4$ cup ($1/2$ stick) butter or margarine, melted
2 cups shredded Swiss cheese

Press the excess moisture from the spinach. Roll the pastry on a lightly floured surface to fit a 9x13-inch baking dish. Fit the pastry over the bottom and up the sides of the dish; trim the edges. Sauté the mushrooms and onion in 2 tablespoons butter in a skillet for 10 minutes. Remove from heat. Stir in the spinach.

Beat the whipping cream, eggs, milk, flour, salt, nutmeg and cayenne pepper in a mixing bowl just until blended. Add $1/4$ cup melted butter and mix well. Layer the spinach mixture, cheese and egg mixture in the pastry-lined baking dish. Bake at 425 degrees for 15 minutes. Reduce the oven temperature to 325 degrees. Bake for 40 minutes longer or until set.

YIELD: 10 SERVINGS

Swiss and Crab Meat Bake

1¼ cups shredded Swiss cheese
1 (6-ounce) can crab meat, drained
2 scallions with tops, finely chopped
1 unbaked (9-inch) pie shell
4 eggs, beaten
1 cup whipping cream
½ teaspoon each dry mustard, grated lemon zest and salt
¼ teaspoon mace
¼ cup sliced almonds, toasted

Layer the cheese, crab meat and scallions in the order listed in the pie shell. Whisk the eggs, whipping cream, dry mustard, zest, salt and mace in a bowl until blended. Pour the egg mixture over the prepared layers. Sprinkle with the almonds. Bake at 325 degrees for 45 minutes or until set.

YIELD: 6 SERVINGS

LIGHTEN UP

Decrease the Swiss cheese to 1 cup and substitute half-and-half or evaporated skim milk for the whipping cream to decrease the fat grams.

Hot-From-the-Oven Tomato Pie

1 (5-count) can biscuits
1 medium onion, finely chopped
2 teaspoons vegetable oil
2 large tomatoes, thinly sliced
1 teaspoon chili powder
½ teaspoon each salt and pepper
⅓ cup mayonnaise
½ cup each shredded Cheddar and mozzarella cheese

Press the biscuits over the bottom and up the side of a greased 9-inch pie plate to form a crust. Sauté the onion in the oil in a skillet until tender. Layer the onion and tomatoes in the prepared pie plate. Sprinkle with the chili powder, salt and pepper.

Combine the mayonnaise, Cheddar cheese and mozzarella cheese in a bowl and mix well. Spread over the prepared layers. Bake at 350 degrees for 35 minutes. Let stand for 10 minutes before serving.

YIELD: 6 SERVINGS

Zucchini and Sausage Pie

Lighten Up

Omit the butter and sauté the zucchini in a nonstick skillet sprayed heavily with nonstick cooking spray. Substitute crisp-cooked chopped Canadian bacon for the sausage, half-and-half for the whipping cream and skim milk for the whole milk.

2 cups shredded unpeeled zucchini
2 tablespoons butter or margarine
8 ounces sweet Italian sausage, casing removed
1 cup shredded Swiss cheese
1 baked (9-inch) pie shell
4 eggs
1 cup milk
$1/2$ cup whipping cream
$1/4$ cup freshly grated Parmesan cheese
$1/2$ teaspoon salt
$1/8$ teaspoon white pepper

Sauté the zucchini in the butter in a skillet for 5 minutes; drain. Brown the sausage in a nonstick skillet, stirring until crumbly; drain. Layer the zucchini, sausage and Swiss cheese in the pie shell.

Beat the eggs in a mixing bowl until blended. Add the milk, whipping cream, Parmesan cheese, salt and white pepper. Beat just until blended. Pour over the prepared layers. Bake at 450 degrees for 15 minutes.

Reduce the oven temperature to 350 degrees. Bake for 30 minutes longer or until a knife inserted near the edge comes out clean. Let stand for several minutes before serving.

YIELD: 6 SERVINGS

WALNUT STREUSEL HOT CRANBERRY CRISP

3 cups whole fresh cranberries
2 cups chopped unpeeled apples
$3/4$ cup sugar
1 tablespoon lemon juice
$1^1/3$ cups quick-cooking oats
1 cup chopped walnuts, toasted
$1/2$ cup packed light brown sugar
$1/2$ cup (1 stick) butter or margarine, melted

Combine the cranberries and apples in a bowl and mix well. Add the sugar and lemon juice and toss to mix. Spoon into a 7x11-inch baking dish sprayed with nonstick cooking spray.

Combine the oats, walnuts and brown sugar in a bowl and mix well. Add the butter, stirring until crumbly. Spread over the cranberries and apples. Bake at 325 degrees for $1^1/4$ hours.

YIELD: 10 SERVINGS

COTTAGE BISCUITS

2 cups unbleached flour
1 cup whole wheat flour
4 teaspoons baking powder
2 teaspoons sugar
1 teaspoon salt
$1/2$ teaspoon baking soda
$1/2$ teaspoon cream of tartar
$1/4$ cup ($1/2$ stick) butter or margarine
$1^1/2$ cups cottage cheese
2 eggs, beaten
2 to 3 tablespoons cornmeal

Mix the flours in a bowl. Stir in the baking powder, sugar, salt, baking soda and cream of tartar. Cut in the butter until crumbly.

Combine the cottage cheese and eggs in a bowl and mix well. Add to the flour mixture and mix well. Turn the dough onto a lightly floured surface. Knead for 1 to 2 minutes. Roll $1/2$ inch thick; cut with a round cutter.

Sprinkle 2 baking sheets with the cornmeal. Arrange the biscuits 2 inches apart on the baking sheets. Bake at 350 degrees for 10 to 12 minutes or until golden brown.

YIELD: 1 $1/2$ DOZEN BISCUITS

ICED PECAN BISCUITS

1 cup chopped pecans
3 (10-count) cans biscuits
1 cup vanilla ice cream
1 cup packed light brown sugar
$1/4$ cup ($1/2$ stick) butter or margarine

Sprinkle the pecans over the bottom of a 9x13-inch baking pan sprayed with nonstick cooking spray. Arrange the biscuits in 3 rows slightly overlapping.

Bring the ice cream, brown sugar and butter to a boil in a saucepan, stirring frequently. Pour over the biscuits. Bake at 400 degrees for 15 minutes. Cool slightly. Invert onto a serving platter.

YIELD: 15 SERVINGS

LIGHTEN UP

Replace frozen vanilla yogurt for the ice cream and margarine for the butter to reduce the cholesterol and fat grams.

APRICOT BREAD

2 teaspoons all-purpose flour
2 cups whole wheat flour
$1/2$ cup packed light brown sugar
2 teaspoons baking soda
$1/2$ teaspoon cinnamon
2 (16-ounce) cans apricots in heavy syrup, drained
2 eggs, lightly beaten
$1/4$ cup corn oil
1 tablespoon vanilla extract

Spray a 5x9-inch loaf pan with nonstick baking spray. Coat the pan with the all-purpose flour. Combine the whole wheat flour, brown sugar, baking soda and cinnamon in a bowl and mix well. Process the apricots in a blender until puréed.

Combine the apricot purée, eggs, corn oil and vanilla in a bowl and mix well. Add the flour mixture, stirring just until moistened. Spoon the batter into the prepared pan. Bake at 350 degrees for 55 minutes or until the loaf tests done. Cool in pan for 10 minutes. Remove to a wire rack to cool completely.

YIELD: 12 SERVINGS

LIGHTEN UP

Substitute apricots in light syrup for the apricots in heavy syrup and replace the eggs with an equal amount of egg substitute.

SUGARLESS BANANA BREAD

2 cups sifted flour
2 teaspoons baking powder
1 teaspoon salt
$1/2$ teaspoon baking soda
$1/2$ teaspoon nutmeg
1 cup mashed banana
$1/3$ cup skim milk
$1/3$ cup vegetable oil
1 egg, lightly beaten
2 teaspoons liquid artificial sweetener

Sift the flour, baking powder, salt, baking soda and nutmeg into a bowl and mix well. Combine the banana, skim milk, oil, egg and artificial sweetener in a bowl and mix well. Add the flour mixture, stirring just until moistened.

Spoon the batter into a greased 5x9-inch loaf pan. Bake at 375 degrees for 50 to 60 minutes or until the loaf tests done. Cool in pan for 10 minutes. Remove to a wire rack to cool completely.

YIELD: 12 SERVINGS

POPPY SEED BREAD WITH LEMON ALMOND GLAZE

3 cups flour
1$^1/_2$ teaspoons baking powder
1$^1/_2$ teaspoons salt
2 cups sugar
1 cup plus 2 tablespoons vegetable oil
3 eggs
2 teaspoons vanilla extract
3 teaspoons almond extract
1$^1/_2$ cups plus 2 tablespoons milk
2 tablespoons poppy seeds
$^3/_4$ cup confectioners' sugar
2 tablespoons butter or margarine, melted
1 teaspoon lemon juice

Sift the flour, baking powder and salt together. Beat the sugar, oil, eggs, 1$^1/_2$ teaspoons of the vanilla, 2$^1/_2$ teaspoons of the almond extract, 1$^1/_2$ cups of the milk and poppy seeds in a mixing bowl until mixed. Add the flour mixture and mix just until moistened. Spoon the batter into 2 greased and floured 5x9-inch loaf pans.

Bake at 350 degrees for 1 hour. Make several slashes in the top of the warm bread with a sharp knife. Run a knife around the edges to loosen.

Combine the confectioners' sugar, butter, lemon juice, remaining $^1/_2$ teaspoon vanilla, remaining $^1/_2$ teaspoon almond extract and remaining 2 tablespoons milk in a bowl and stir until of the consistency of a glaze. Pour over the warm loaves. Remove to a wire rack to cool completely.

YIELD: 24 SERVINGS

LIGHTEN UP

Omit the Lemon Almond Glaze and sprinkle with 2 tablespoons sifted confectioners' sugar. Substitute skim milk for the whole milk.

SUN-DRIED TOMATO BREAD

$2^{1}/_{2}$ cups flour
$2^{1}/_{2}$ teaspoons baking powder
$2^{1}/_{2}$ teaspoons salt
1 cup shredded provolone cheese
$^{1}/_{3}$ cup drained oil-packed sun-dried tomatoes, chopped
$^{1}/_{3}$ cup chopped green onions
2 tablespoons minced fresh parsley
2 teaspoons rosemary
$^{1}/_{2}$ teaspoon freshly ground pepper
$1^{1}/_{4}$ cups buttermilk
2 tablespoons vegetable oil
2 tablespoons sugar
2 garlic cloves, minced
2 eggs

Combine the flour, baking powder and salt in a bowl and mix well. Stir in the cheese, sun-dried tomatoes, green onions, parsley, rosemary and pepper. Whisk the buttermilk, oil, sugar, garlic and eggs in a bowl until mixed. Add to the flour mixture, stirring just until moistened.

Spoon the batter into a greased 5x9-inch loaf pan. Bake at 350 degrees for 1 hour or until the loaf tests done. Cool in pan for 10 minutes. Remove to a wire rack to cool to the desired temperature. Serve warm or at room temperature.

YIELD: 12 SERVINGS

WHOLE WHEAT GARDEN MUFFINS

1³/₄ cups all-purpose flour
1³/₄ cups whole wheat flour
1¹/₂ teaspoons baking soda
1 teaspoon salt
³/₄ teaspoon baking powder
³/₄ teaspoon cinnamon
3 eggs
1 cup sugar
1 cup vegetable oil
³/₄ cup packed light brown sugar
1³/₄ cups shredded yellow squash or zucchini
1 small carrot, shredded
1 cup vanilla reduced-fat yogurt

Combine the all-purpose flour, whole wheat flour, baking soda, salt, baking powder and cinnamon in a bowl and mix well. Beat the eggs in a mixing bowl until blended. Add the sugar, oil and brown sugar. Beat until smooth. Fold in the flour mixture. Add the squash, carrot and yogurt.

Beat at medium speed just until mixed, scraping the bowl occasionally; do not overbeat. Spoon the batter into muffin cups sprayed with nonstick cooking spray. Bake at 350 degrees for 15 to 20 minutes or until the muffins test done.

YIELD: 2 DOZEN MUFFINS

CHEDDAR MUFFINS WITH APPLE BUTTER

R_X FACTS ABOUT AVOIDING ASTHMA

To avoid asthma triggers or decrease asthma attacks:

✳ *Remove animal hair.*

✳ *Dust regularly.*

✳ *Vacuum carpet regularly.*

✳ *Use a HEPA filter to keep your home allergen-free.*

APPLE BUTTER

1/2 cup (1 stick) butter, softened
1/2 cup apple jelly
1/4 to 1/2 teaspoon cinnamon

MUFFINS

2 cups flour
1/2 cup sugar
1 tablespoon baking powder
1/2 teaspoon baking soda
1/2 teaspoon salt
2 cups shredded sharp Cheddar cheese
1 cup plain yogurt
1/4 cup (1/2 stick) butter or margarine, melted
2 eggs, beaten

To prepare the apple butter, beat the butter in a mixing bowl until creamy. Add the jelly and cinnamon. Beat until blended.

To prepare the muffins, combine the flour, sugar, baking powder, baking soda and salt in a bowl and mix well. Stir in the cheese. Make a well in the center of the flour mixture.

Whisk the yogurt, butter and eggs in a bowl until blended. Add to the well and stir just until moistened; the batter will be thick. Fill greased muffin cups 2/3 full. Bake on the center oven rack at 400 degrees for 14 minutes or until the muffins test done. Serve with Apple Butter.

YIELD: 1 DOZEN MUFFINS

FEEL-NO-GUILT BANANA CRUNCH MUFFINS

1 cup flour
1/2 cup sugar
1/2 cup Grape-Nuts cereal
1/2 teaspoon baking soda
1/2 teaspoon baking powder
1/4 teaspoon salt
1 large banana, mashed
1/2 cup plain yogurt
1/4 cup frozen egg substitute, thawed
1/2 teaspoon vanilla extract

Combine the flour, sugar, cereal, baking soda, baking powder and salt in a bowl and mix well. Combine the banana, yogurt, egg substitute and vanilla in a bowl and mix well. Add to the flour mixture, stirring just until moistened.

Spoon the batter into muffin cups sprayed with nonstick cooking spray. Bake at 350 degrees for 20 minutes or until the muffins test done.

YIELD: 1 DOZEN MUFFINS

CRÈME BRÛLÉE FRENCH TOAST

LIGHTEN UP

Use 1 1/2 cups evaporated skim milk for the half-and-half, and the equivalent amount of egg substitute for the eggs.

1/2 cup (1 stick) unsalted butter or margarine
1 cup packed light brown sugar
1/4 cup corn syrup
12 (1-inch-thick) slices crusty Italian bread, crusts trimmed
1 1/2 cups half-and-half
6 eggs
1 teaspoon vanilla extract
1 teaspoon Grand Marnier
1/4 teaspoon salt

Combine the butter, brown sugar and corn syrup in a saucepan. Cook over medium heat until blended, stirring constantly. Pour into a 9x13-inch baking pan. Arrange the bread slices in a single layer in the prepared baking pan; the slices will fit very snug.

Whisk the half-and-half, eggs, vanilla, Grand Marnier and salt in a bowl until blended. Pour over the bread. Chill, covered, for 8 to 24 hours. Bring the bread mixture to room temperature. Bake on the center oven rack at 350 degrees for 35 to 40 minutes or until puffed and light brown.

YIELD: 6 (2-SLICE) SERVINGS

GUILTLESS STUFFED FRENCH TOAST

8 slices reduced-calorie bread, cubed
2 cups reduced-fat ricotta cheese
1/3 cup reduced-calorie syrup
2 cups frozen egg substitute, thawed
2 cups skim milk
1/4 teaspoon cinnamon

Arrange half the bread cubes in a greased 8x8-inch baking pan. Combine the ricotta cheese and 1/3 of the syrup in a bowl and mix well. Spread the cheese mixture over the bread cubes. Top with the remaining bread cubes. Combine the remaining syrup, egg substitute, skim milk and cinnamon in a bowl and mix well. Pour over the prepared layers.

Chill, covered, for 8 to 10 hours. Bake at 375 degrees for 45 minutes. Let stand for 15 minutes before serving. Cut into 8 squares.

YIELD: 8 SERVINGS

WHOLE WHEAT BUTTERMILK WAFFLES

1 cup all-purpose flour
3/4 cup whole wheat flour
2 teaspoons baking powder
1/2 teaspoon salt
1/2 teaspoon baking soda
2 cups buttermilk
1/2 cup vegetable oil
2 egg yolks
2 egg whites, stiffly beaten

Sift the all-purpose flour, whole wheat flour, baking powder, salt and baking soda into a bowl and mix well. Beat the buttermilk, oil and egg yolks in a mixing bowl until blended. Add to the dry ingredients and mix just until moistened. Fold in the egg whites.

Pour 1/6 of the batter onto a hot lightly greased waffle iron. Bake until brown on both sides using manufacturer's directions. Repeat the process with the remaining batter.

YIELD: 6 WAFFLES

Rx FACTS ABOUT MEDICATIONS

Be sure to know why your medicine has been prescribed and what it's supposed to do. Don't hesitate to ask questions that concern you. If you are unsure what the medical problem is, ask your pharmacist to talk with your physician.

OVEN PUFF WITH STRAWBERRY SAUCE

LIGHTEN UP

Use skim milk for the whole milk, decrease the butter to 6 tablespoons and substitute nonfat sour cream for the sour cream.

1 cup milk
6 eggs
1 cup flour
$1/2$ cup sugar
6 tablespoons orange juice
$1/4$ teaspoon salt
$1/2$ cup (1 stick) butter or margarine
1 (10-ounce) package frozen strawberries in syrup, thawed
$1/4$ cup sifted confectioners' sugar
$1/4$ cup sour cream

Beat the milk and eggs in a mixing bowl until blended. Add the flour, sugar, 4 tablespoons of the orange juice and salt. Beat until smooth.

Heat the butter in a 9x13-inch baking pan in a 425-degree oven until the butter sizzles; do not brown. Pour the batter into the prepared baking pan. Bake on the middle oven rack for 20 minutes or until puffed and brown.

Heat the undrained strawberries and remaining 2 tablespoons orange juice in a saucepan over low heat until heated through, stirring occasionally. Sprinkle the puff with the confectioners' sugar. Serve with the warm strawberry sauce and sour cream.

YIELD: 6 SERVINGS

CREAM CHEESE POPOVERS

1 1/2 cups flour
6 eggs
1 teaspoon salt
1 teaspoon thyme
1/2 teaspoon pepper
1/8 teaspoon nutmeg
2 cups 2% milk
1/4 cup reduced-fat whipping cream
4 ounces nonfat cream cheese, cut into 12 cubes

Spray 12 nonstick muffin cups with nonstick cooking spray. Heat in a 400-degree oven until slightly warm. Combine the flour, eggs, salt, thyme, pepper and nutmeg in a blender container. Process until blended. Add the 2% milk and whipping cream. Process until smooth.

Fill the warm muffin cups 1/2 full with the batter. Place 1 cube of the cream cheese in the center of each cup. Top with the remaining batter.

Bake at 400 degrees for 40 minutes or until puffed and light brown. Serve immediately.

YIELD: 12 POPOVERS

SWEET ENDINGS

APPLE LASAGNA

1 cup sour cream
$1/3$ cup packed plus 6 tablespoons brown sugar
2 cups shredded Cheddar cheese
1 cup ricotta cheese
$1/4$ cup sugar
1 egg, lightly beaten
1 teaspoon almond extract
2 (21-ounce) cans apple pie filling
8 lasagna noodles, cooked, rinsed, drained
6 tablespoons flour
$1/4$ cup quick-cooking oats
1 teaspoon cinnamon
$1/8$ teaspoon nutmeg
3 tablespoons butter or margarine

Combine the sour cream and $1/3$ cup of the brown sugar in a small bowl and mix well. Chill, covered, until serving time. Combine the Cheddar cheese, ricotta cheese, sugar, egg and flavoring in a bowl and mix well.

Spread 1 can of the pie filling in a lightly greased 9x13-inch baking dish. Layer half the noodles, Cheddar cheese mixture, remaining noodles and remaining can of pie filling in the prepared dish.

Combine the remaining 6 tablespoons of brown sugar, flour, oats, cinnamon and nutmeg in a bowl and mix well. Cut in the butter until crumbly. Sprinkle over the prepared layers. Bake at 350 degrees for 45 minutes or until bubbly.

Cut the lasagna into 15 squares. Top each square with a dollop of the sour cream mixture. Serve immediately.

YIELD: 15 SERVINGS

Apricot Pecan Tassies

Pastry

1 cup flour
1/2 cup (1 stick) butter or margarine, chopped
6 tablespoons reduced-fat cream cheese

Apricot Filling

3/4 cup packed brown sugar
1 egg, lightly beaten
1 tablespoon butter or margarine, softened
1/2 teaspoon vanilla extract
1/4 teaspoon salt
2/3 cup dried apricots, finely chopped
1/2 cup finely chopped pecans, toasted

To prepare the pastry, combine the flour, butter and cream cheese in a food processor container. Process until the mixture forms a ball. Chill, wrapped in plastic wrap, for 15 minutes. Shape the dough into twenty-four 1-inch balls. Press each ball over the bottom and up the side of a miniature muffin cup.

To prepare the filling, combine the brown sugar, egg, butter, vanilla and salt in a mixing bowl. Beat until blended. Stir in the apricots and pecans. Spoon into the pastry-lined muffin cups. Bake at 325 degrees for 25 minutes or until set. Cool in pans on a wire rack.

Yield: 2 dozen tassies

LIME CHEESECAKE

LIGHTEN UP

Omit the crust. Use reduced-fat or nonfat cream cheese for the cream cheese. Omit the butter and substitute 8 ounces reduced-fat whipped topping for the whipping cream. Spoon into dessert goblets.

GRAHAM CRACKER CRUST

1 cup graham cracker crumbs
$1/4$ cup sugar
$1/3$ cup butter or margarine, melted

LIME FILLING

1 cup lime juice
$1/4$ cup water
2 envelopes unflavored gelatin
$1^1/2$ cups sugar
5 eggs, lightly beaten
1 tablespoon grated lime zest
16 ounces cream cheese, softened
$1/2$ cup (1 stick) butter or margarine, softened
$1/2$ cup whipping cream
1 lime, thinly sliced

To prepare the crust, combine the graham cracker crumbs, sugar and butter in a bowl and mix well. Press the crumb mixture over the bottom and up the side of a greased 9-inch springform pan.

To prepare the filling, combine the lime juice, water and unflavored gelatin in a saucepan and mix well. Let stand for 5 minutes or until the gelatin is softened. Stir in the sugar, eggs and zest. Cook over medium heat for 6 to 7 minutes or just until the mixture comes to a boil, stirring constantly; do not boil. Remove from heat.

Beat the cream cheese and butter in a mixing bowl until smooth, scraping the bowl occasionally. Add the gelatin mixture gradually, beating constantly until blended. Chill, covered, for 1 hour, stirring occasionally.

Beat the whipping cream in a mixing bowl until stiff peaks form. Fold into the cream cheese mixture. Spread in the prepared pan. Chill, covered, for $1^1/2$ to 3 hours or until firm. Remove the side of the pan. Place the cheesecake on a cake plate. Arrange the lime slices in a decorative pattern over the top.

YIELD: 12 SERVINGS

PECAN-TOPPED FUDGE CHEESECAKE

PECAN CRUST

1 cup graham cracker crumbs
$1/4$ cup ground pecans
$1/4$ cup ($1/2$ stick) butter or margarine, melted
3 tablespoons brown sugar
$1/2$ teaspoon cinnamon

FUDGE FILLING

24 ounces cream cheese, softened
$3/4$ cup packed brown sugar
$1/2$ cup sugar
2 tablespoons flour
3 eggs
1 cup sour cream
2 ounces unsweetened chocolate, melted
1 tablespoon butter or margarine, melted
$1/2$ cup chopped pecans, toasted

To prepare the crust, combine the graham cracker crumbs, pecans, butter, brown sugar and cinnamon in a bowl and mix well. Press over the bottom and up the side of a greased 9-inch springform pan. Bake at 350 degrees for 10 minutes. Let stand until cool.

To prepare the filling, combine the cream cheese, $1/2$ cup of the brown sugar, sugar and flour in a mixing bowl. Beat until smooth, scraping the bowl occasionally. Add the eggs 1 at a time, beating well after each addition. Add the sour cream and chocolate and beat until blended. Spread in the prepared pan.

Bake at 425 degrees for 10 minutes. Reduce the oven temperature to 250 degrees. Sprinkle with a mixture of the remaining $1/4$ cup brown sugar, butter and pecans. Bake for 45 minutes longer or until set. Loosen the side of the pan. Cool in pan on a wire rack. Chill, covered, until serving time.

YIELD: 12 SERVINGS

PEACH BLUEBERRY CRISP

6 cups sliced peeled fresh peaches
2 cups fresh blueberries
$1/3$ cup plus $1/4$ cup packed brown sugar
2 tablespoons flour
3 teaspoons cinnamon
1 cup quick-cooking oats
3 tablespoons butter or margarine

Toss the peaches and blueberries in a bowl. Combine $1/3$ cup of the brown sugar, flour and 2 teaspoons of the cinnamon in a bowl and mix well. Add to the peach mixture and toss to coat. Spoon into a 7x11-inch baking dish.

Combine the remaining $1/4$ cup brown sugar, remaining 1 teaspoon cinnamon and oats in a bowl and mix well. Add the butter and stir until crumbly. Sprinkle over the peach mixture.

Bake at 350 degrees for 25 minutes or until the fruit is tender and crisp is bubbly. Serve hot, warm or chilled with frozen vanilla yogurt. For variety, substitute sliced peeled apples for the peaches and blackberries for the blueberries.

YIELD: 8 SERVINGS

BERRY TRIFLE

4 cups frozen strawberries, thawed, drained
$^1/_4$ cup sugar
1 (1-pound) pound cake, cubed
$^1/_2$ cup sherry
2 cups frozen blueberries, thawed, drained
2 cups frozen sliced peaches, thawed, drained
3 cups vanilla pudding
$^1/_2$ cup slivered almonds, toasted
1 cup whipping cream
2 tablespoons superfine sugar
$^1/_4$ teaspoon vanilla extract

LIGHTEN UP

Substitute a 1-pound angel food cake for the pound cake. Omit the whipping cream, superfine sugar and vanilla and substitute with 2 to 2$^1/_2$ cups reduced-fat whipped topping.

Process 1 cup of the strawberries and $^1/_4$ cup sugar in a blender until puréed. Line a 3-quart glass trifle bowl with half the pound cake cubes. Drizzle with half the sherry. Pour half the strawberry purée over the cake. Sprinkle 1 cup of the strawberries, 1 cup of the blueberries and 1 cup of the peaches in the prepared bowl. Spread with half the pudding and sprinkle with half the almonds. Layer the remaining cake, remaining sherry, remaining strawberry purée, remaining strawberries, remaining blueberries, remaining peaches, remaining pudding and remaining almonds in the order listed over the prepared layers.

Beat the whipping cream, 2 tablespoons superfine sugar and vanilla in a mixing bowl until stiff peaks form, scraping the bowl occasionally. Spread over the top. Garnish with additional fresh berries. Chill, covered, until serving time.

YIELD: 12 SERVINGS

POACHED PEARS WITH RASPBERRY SAUCE

PEARS

4 large ripe pears, peeled, cored
4 cups apple juice
2 tablespoons sugar
1 cinnamon stick
1 teaspoon grated orange zest
1/2 teaspoon grated lemon zest
1/4 teaspoon ground cloves

RASPBERRY SAUCE

1 pint fresh raspberries
3 tablespoons sugar
1 teaspoon Grand Marnier

To prepare the pears, cut a small slice from the bottom of each pear so the pears will stand upright. Combine the apple juice, sugar, cinnamon stick, zests and cloves in a large saucepan and mix well. Bring to a boil over medium heat; reduce heat to low.

Simmer for 5 minutes, stirring occasionally. Stand the pears in the liquid. Poach, covered, for 20 minutes or until the pears are tender. Remove from heat. Let the pears stand in the poaching liquid until cool. Chill, covered, in the poaching liquid until serving time.

To prepare the sauce, toss the raspberries with the sugar and Grand Marnier in a bowl. Let stand at room temperature for 1 hour. Transfer the raspberry mixture to a food processor container. Process until puréed. You may store the sauce, covered, in the refrigerator for 2 to 4 weeks or in the freezer for 3 to 4 months.

To assemble, remove the pears from the poaching liquid to 4 dessert plates with a slotted spoon. Drizzle with the sauce. Garnish with mint leaves.

YIELD: 4 SERVINGS

Italian Strawberry Ice

2 cups sugar
1 cup water
2 quarts fresh strawberries
$1/3$ cup orange juice
$1/4$ cup lemon juice
$3 1/3$ cups California pink Champagne

Combine the sugar and water in a medium saucepan. Cook until the sugar dissolves, stirring occasionally. Bring to a boil. Boil for 5 minutes. Remove from heat. Let stand until cool.

Process the strawberries in a blender until puréed. Stir the strawberry purée, orange juice and lemon juice into the sugar syrup. Pour into ice cube trays. Wrap the trays in foil. Freeze until firm.

Remove the trays 20 minutes before serving to allow the ice to thaw slightly. Scoop into dessert goblets. Pour $1/3$ cup of the Champagne into each goblet. Serve immediately.

YIELD: 10 SERVINGS

DECADENT TRUFFLES

1^1/$_3$ cups whipping cream
^{1}/$_4$ cup packed brown sugar
2 teaspoons vanilla extract
^{1}/$_4$ teaspoon salt
16 ounces milk chocolate, chopped
16 ounces semisweet chocolate, chopped
1 cup finely chopped pecans, lightly toasted
1 cup shredded coconut, lightly toasted (optional)

Combine the whipping cream, brown sugar, vanilla and salt in a saucepan and mix well. Cook over medium heat until the brown sugar dissolves and the mixture is hot, stirring constantly. Remove from heat. Add the milk chocolate and semisweet chocolate, stirring until smooth. You may return to the heat if necessary to melt the chocolate.

Spoon the chocolate mixture into a shallow dish. Chill, covered, for 1 to 2 hours or until firm. Shape into 1-inch balls. Roll in the pecans and coconut. Store, covered, in the refrigerator or freeze for future use.

YIELD: 72 TRUFFLES

MIRACULOUSLY EASY PRALINES

1 cup whipping cream
1 (1-pound) package light brown sugar
2 cups broken pecans, toasted
2 tablespoons butter or margarine, melted
1 teaspoon vanilla extract

Combine the whipping cream and brown sugar in a microwave-safe bowl and mix well. Microwave on High for 8 to 12 minutes or until the mixture comes to a boil. Stir in the pecans, butter and vanilla.

Drop by spoonfuls onto a foil-lined tray immediately. Let stand until firm.

YIELD: 3 DOZEN PRALINES

ALMOND JOY CAKE

CAKE

2 cups flour
2 cups sugar
1 cup water
$1/2$ cup (1 stick) butter or margarine
$1/2$ cup shortening
$3^1/2$ tablespoons baking cocoa
$1/2$ cup buttermilk
2 eggs, lightly beaten
1 teaspoon baking soda
1 teaspoon vanilla extract
$1/2$ teaspoon salt

COCONUT FILLING

1 cup sugar
1 cup evaporated milk
24 large marshmallows
1 (7-ounce) package shredded coconut

CHOCOLATE TOPPING

$1/2$ cup (1 stick) butter or margarine
2 cups semisweet chocolate chips
1 cup slivered almonds

To prepare the cake, combine the flour and sugar in a bowl and mix well. Combine the water, butter, shortening and baking cocoa in a saucepan. Bring to a boil, stirring frequently. Pour over the flour mixture and mix well. Whisk the buttermilk, eggs, baking soda, vanilla and salt in a bowl until blended. Add to the cocoa mixture and mix well. Spoon the batter into a greased 9x13-inch cake pan. Bake at 350 degrees for 40 to 45 minutes or until the cake tests done.

To prepare the filling, combine the sugar, evaporated milk and marshmallows in a saucepan. Cook over medium-low heat until blended, stirring constantly. Stir in the coconut. Spread over the hot cake.

To prepare the topping, heat the butter and chocolate chips in a saucepan over low heat until blended, stirring frequently. Add the almonds and mix well. Spread over the filling.

YIELD: 15 SERVINGS

LIGHTEN UP

Make into 24 cupcakes and substitute evaporated skim milk for the evaporated milk.

GRANDMA'S TRADITIONAL APPLE CAKE

Sander Walker of ARROW 93.7 in Sacramento, California, donated this recipe.

2 cups sugar
1^1/$_2$ cups vegetable oil
2 eggs, lightly beaten
1^1/$_2$ teaspoons cinnamon
1 teaspoon vanilla extract
^{1}/$_2$ teaspoon salt
3 cups flour
3 large red apples, peeled, cut into 1-inch pieces
1 cup chopped pecans or walnuts

Combine the sugar, oil, eggs, cinnamon, vanilla and salt in a bowl and mix well. Stir in the flour. Add the apples and pecans and mix well.

Spoon the batter into a greased and floured 10-inch tube pan; smooth top. Bake at 325 degrees for 1^1/$_2$ to 2 hours or until a knife inserted near the center comes out clean. Cool in the pan on a wire rack. Remove to a serving platter.

YIELD: 12 SERVINGS

TROPICAL CARROT CAKE

CAKE

1 1/2 cups plus 1 teaspoon unbleached flour
1/4 cup wheat germ
2 teaspoons baking powder
2 teaspoons baking soda
1 1/2 teaspoons cinnamon
1/2 teaspoon nutmeg
1/4 teaspoon salt
1 cup packed light brown sugar
1 cup frozen egg substitute, thawed
1 cup plain nonfat yogurt
1 teaspoon vanilla extract
1 cup raisins
1 3/4 cups shredded carrots
1 (8-ounce) can juice-packed crushed pineapple, drained

CREAM CHEESE FROSTING

4 ounces reduced-fat cream cheese, softened
1 1/2 cups confectioners' sugar
2 teaspoons lemon juice
1 teaspoon vanilla extract

To prepare the cake, combine 1 1/2 cups flour, wheat germ, baking powder, baking soda, cinnamon, nutmeg and salt in a bowl and mix well. Beat the brown sugar, egg substitute, yogurt and vanilla in a mixing bowl until blended, scraping the bowl occasionally. Add the flour mixture gradually and beat just until moistened.

Coat the raisins with the remaining 1 teaspoon flour in a bowl. Fold the raisins, carrots and pineapple into the batter. Spoon the batter into a 9x13-inch cake pan sprayed with nonstick cooking spray. Bake at 350 degrees for 30 to 40 minutes or until the cake tests done. Cool in the pan on a wire rack.

To prepare the frosting, beat the cream cheese in a mixing bowl until creamy. Add the confectioners' sugar gradually, beating constantly at low speed until smooth. Add the lemon juice and vanilla. Beat until of a spreading consistency. Spread over the top of the cooled cake.

YIELD: 15 SERVINGS

CHOCOLATE PECAN TORTE CAKE

RECIPE FOR CHOCOLATE GLAZE

Combine 1/2 cup water, 3 ounces coarsely chopped semisweet chocolate, 6 table-spoons unsalted butter and 3 tablespoons vegetable oil in a double boiler over simmering water. Simmer until the chocolate melts, stirring frequently. Remove from heat. Add 3/4 cup baking cocoa and 1/2 cup plus 2 tablespoons sugar, stirring until the sugar dissolves. Cool until slightly thickened or of a drizzling consistency.

CAKE

3/4 cup (11/2 sticks) unsalted butter
2 cups sugar
8 eggs
2 tablespoons vanilla extract
1/4 teaspoon salt
12 ounces semisweet chocolate, melted
31/2 cups finely ground pecans

STRAWBERRY BUTTERCREAM FROSTING

2 cups confectioners' sugar, sifted
11/4 cups (21/2 sticks) unsalted butter, softened
4 egg yolks, beaten, or equivalent amount of egg substitute
1/2 cup puréed strawberries
3 tablespoons strawberry preserves

CHOCOLATE GLAZE (in sidebar)

To prepare the cake, coat the sides and bottoms of four 9-inch cake pans with butter. Line the bottoms with baking parchment; coat the parchment with butter. Beat 3/4 cup butter in a mixing bowl until creamy. Add the sugar. Beat until light and fluffy. Add the eggs 1 at a time, beating well after each addition. Beat in the vanilla and salt. Fold in the chocolate and pecans. Spoon the batter into the prepared pans.

Bake at 375 degrees for 22 minutes or until a wooden pick inserted in the center comes out fudgy but not wet. Cool in pans on a wire rack for 5 minutes. Run a sharp knife around the edges of the pans to loosen the layers. Invert onto a wire rack to cool completely.

To prepare the frosting, beat the confectioners' sugar and butter in a mixing bowl until light and fluffy. Add the egg yolks, strawberry purée and preserves and mix well. Chill, covered, until set. Bring to room temperature before using. To avoid raw eggs that may carry salmonella we suggest using an equivalent amount of commercial egg substitute.

To assemble, stack the cake layers bottom side up on a cake plate spreading about 2/3 cup of the frosting between each layer. Chill, covered, for 6 hours or longer. Drizzle the glaze over the top allowing it to flow down the side. Let stand at room temperature for 1 hour before serving.

YIELD: 16 SERVINGS

Chocolate Intimidator

Cake

1 pound semisweet chocolate, coarsely chopped
2 cups (4 sticks) butter
1 cup sugar
1 cup half-and-half
1 tablespoon vanilla extract
$1/8$ teaspoon salt
6 eggs

Chocolate Glaze

6 ounces semisweet chocolate, coarsely chopped
3 tablespoons butter
2 tablespoons half-and-half
2 tablespoons light corn syrup

To prepare the cake, line the bottom of a 9-inch springform pan with foil. Coat the foil and side of the pan with butter. Combine the chocolate, butter, sugar, half-and-half, vanilla and salt in a saucepan. Cook over low heat until blended, stirring frequently. Whisk the eggs in a bowl until blended. Add a small amount of the warm chocolate mixture gradually to the eggs and whisk until smooth. Stir in the remaining warm chocolate mixture and mix until smooth.

Spoon the batter into the prepared pan. Bake at 350 degrees for 40 to 45 minutes or until a wooden pick inserted in a 2-inch area around the edge comes out clean; the middle will look unbaked. Cool in pan on a wire rack; the center may crack as it cools. Chill, covered, in the refrigerator.

To prepare the glaze, combine the chocolate and butter in a double boiler over hot water. Simmer until blended, stirring frequently. Add the half-and-half and corn syrup and mix well. Simmer just until heated through and of a glaze consistency, stirring constantly.

To assemble, remove the side of the pan. Place the cake on a cake plate. Drizzle with the glaze. Chill until the glaze is set. Top with whipped cream and/or fresh raspberries.

Yield: 12 servings

BRICKLE CRUNCH COOKIES

3¹/₂ cups all-purpose flour
1 cup whole wheat flour
1 teaspoon baking soda
1 teaspoon salt
1 teaspoon cream of tartar
1 cup confectioners' sugar
1 cup plus ¹/₂ cup sugar
1 cup (2 sticks) butter or margarine, softened
1 cup vegetable oil
2 eggs
1 teaspoon almond extract
2 cups coarsely chopped almonds
1 cup almond brickle chips

Combine the all-purpose flour, whole wheat flour, baking soda, salt and cream of tartar in a bowl and mix well. Beat the confectioners' sugar, 1 cup of the sugar, butter and oil in a mixing bowl until smooth, scraping the bowl occasionally. Add the eggs and extract and mix well. Add the flour mixture gradually, beating at low speed after each addition until blended. Stir in the almonds and brickle chips. Chill, covered, until firm.

Shape the dough by large tablespoonfuls into balls. Roll in the remaining ¹/₂ cup sugar. Arrange 3 inches apart on an ungreased cookie sheet. Flatten with a fork dipped in sugar. Bake at 350 degrees for 12 to 18 minutes or until brown around the edges. Cool on cookie sheet for 2 minutes. Remove to a wire rack to cool completely.

YIELD: 6 DOZEN COOKIES

FUDGE SUNDAE COOKIES

1 1/4 cups flour
3/4 teaspoon baking soda
1/2 teaspoon salt
1/2 cup (1 stick) butter or margarine, softened
1/2 cup creamy peanut butter
1/2 cup sugar
1/2 cup packed brown sugar
1 egg
2 teaspoons vanilla extract
1 (14-ounce) can sweetened condensed milk
1 cup milk chocolate chips
1 cup semisweet chocolate chips
1/2 cup chopped peanuts

Combine the flour, baking soda and salt in a bowl and mix well. Cream the butter, peanut butter, sugar and brown sugar in a mixing bowl until creamy. Add the egg and 1 teaspoon of the vanilla. Beat until light and fluffy. Stir in the dry ingredients. Chill, covered, for 1 hour.

Shape the dough into 1-inch balls. Place each ball in a lightly greased miniature muffin cup. Bake at 325 degrees for 14 to 16 minutes or until light brown. Make an indentation in the center of each.

Combine the condensed milk, milk chocolate chips and semisweet chocolate chips in a saucepan. Cook over low heat until blended, stirring frequently. Stir in the remaining 1 teaspoon vanilla. Spoon the chocolate sauce into the indentations. Sprinkle with the peanuts.

YIELD: 4 DOZEN COOKIES

WHITE CHOCOLATE BISCOTTI

2 cups plus 2 tablespoons flour
$1^{1}/_{2}$ teaspoons baking powder
$^{1}/_{4}$ teaspoon salt
$^{1}/_{4}$ teaspoon baking soda
$^{1}/_{2}$ cup (1 stick) butter, softened
$^{3}/_{4}$ cup sugar
2 eggs
2 tablespoons amaretto
1 teaspoon vanilla extract
$^{2}/_{3}$ cup chopped almonds
$^{2}/_{3}$ cup white chocolate chips

Combine the flour, baking powder, salt and baking soda in a bowl and mix well. Beat the butter and sugar in a mixing bowl until light and fluffy. Add the eggs, amaretto and vanilla. Beat until blended. Stir in the dry ingredients. Fold in the almonds and chocolate chips.

Divide the dough into 2 equal portions. Shape each portion into a log, 14 inches long and $^{1}/_{2}$ inch thick. Arrange the logs 2 inches apart on a greased and floured cookie sheet.

Bake on the middle oven rack at 325 degrees for 25 minutes. Cool on the cookie sheet for 5 minutes. Cut the logs into $^{1}/_{2}$-inch slices. Arrange the slices cut side down on the cookie sheet. Bake for 8 minutes longer. Remove to a wire rack to cool. Store in an airtight container.

YIELD: 3 DOZEN BISCOTTI

LEMON COCONUT BARS

1 1/2 cups plus 2 tablespoons flour
1 1/2 cups packed light brown sugar
1/2 cup (1 stick) butter or margarine, softened
2 eggs
1 1/2 cups shredded coconut
1 cup chopped pecans
1/2 teaspoon baking powder
1/2 teaspoon vanilla extract
1/4 teaspoon salt
1 cup confectioners' sugar
1 tablespoon butter or margarine, melted
Juice of 1 lemon

Combine 1 1/2 cups of the flour, 1/2 cup of the brown sugar and 1/2 cup butter in a medium bowl and mix well. Press over the bottom of a greased 9x13-inch baking pan. Bake at 275 degrees for 10 minutes. Remove from oven.

Beat the eggs in a mixing bowl until blended. Add the remaining 1 cup brown sugar, remaining 2 tablespoons flour, coconut, pecans, baking powder, vanilla and salt and mix well. Spread over the baked layer. Bake at 350 degrees for 20 minutes.

Combine the confectioners' sugar, 1 tablespoon melted butter and lemon juice in a medium mixing bowl. Beat until of a spreading consistency. Spread the glaze over the warm baked layer. Cool in pan on a wire rack. Cut into bars.

YIELD: 2 DOZEN BARS

Rx FACTS ABOUT WEIGHT LOSS

Using certain weight loss agents such as fat blockers (Xenical®), may increase your daily vitamin requirements due to depletion of fat-soluble vitamins (i.e. Vitamins A, E, D and K). Make sure to ask your pharmacist if you should take extra supplements.

LEMON SHORTBREAD WITH WHITE CHOCOLATE GLAZE

$1/2$ cup hazelnuts or pecan halves
1 cup flour
$1/2$ cup confectioners' sugar
$1/2$ cup (1 stick) butter or margarine, softened
$1/4$ cup cornstarch
2 teaspoons grated lemon zest
1 egg yolk
$1/4$ teaspoon salt
$1/8$ teaspoon nutmeg
4 ounces white chocolate coating, melted

Line a 9x9-inch baking pan with foil, allowing a 1-inch overhang. Spray the foil with nonstick cooking spray.

Spread the hazelnuts in a single layer on a baking sheet. Toast at 375 degrees for 7 to 8 minutes. Reduce the oven temperature to 325 degrees. Rub the hazelnuts with a tea towel to remove the skins. Chop the hazelnuts in a food processor until medium-fine. Add the flour, confectioners' sugar, butter, cornstarch, zest, egg yolk, salt and nutmeg. Process until crumbly.

Press the crumb mixture evenly into the prepared pan. Bake at 325 degrees for 25 to 30 minutes or until light brown. Cool in pan on a wire rack for 10 minutes. Lift the shortbread out of the pan using the foil. Cut into diamonds. Remove to a wire rack to cool. Drizzle with the white chocolate coating. Let stand until set. Store in a cool environment in an airtight container for up to 2 weeks.

YIELD: 1 DOZEN

The Art of Growing
Edible Flowers and Herbs

Allium

A perennial herb that blooms during May and June with pretty lilac-pink flowers that can be used, in addition to the hollow leaves, as a garnish or substitute for scallions. It is a hardy plant that imparts an onion flavor to fish dishes, soups, salads, creamed cheeses, or white vinegar.

Anise Hyssop

Used in soups, baked goods, tea, and sugar and complementary with cinnamon and bay leaves, it is a perennial herb. Native Americans used the licorice-tasting leaves as a sweetener and the roots as a cough remedy. This self-sowing plant should be planted in mid-spring to bloom dusky indigo spikes in July.

Basil

The leaf harvest is increased if the leaves are picked before the white-pale pink flowers open. After the leaves are picked they should be kept in an airtight container unwashed, since water blackens the leaves. An annual herb that can be used on pizza or with a variety of meats, fowl, and vegetables, and combined with butter, vinegar, or oil, imparting a sweet flavor with a suggestion of mint and clove.

Bee Balm

Bees and hummingbirds are also attracted to this citrus-tasting herb with its leaves and flowers that can be used with fruits, duck, and pork or in salads, teas, and jellies. A tall, stately perennial with fuzzy leaves that can be picked anytime and colorful scarlet flowers, bee balm has quick-spreading roots and should be divided and replanted in the fall.

Borage

Both the leaves and bright blue star-shaped flowers have a cucumber-like flavor and are often used in salads, but the flowers may also be floated in drinks or candied for a dessert garnish. It can be grown from seeds planted in early May. Use the leaves sparingly as large amounts may be toxic. Both flowers and leaves store poorly and should be used fresh.

Burnet

Often substituted for cucumbers in salads. Burnet needs to be used fresh as it loses its flavor when dried. This perennial should be planted in poor, sandy, slightly alkaline soil and lightly watered and fertilized. It blooms in July with dense tufts of white to raspberry-colored flowers.

Calendula

The ray petal is the edible portion of the yellow-orange blossom and provides an attractive garnish. It is often used to tint butter and cheese and is commonly known as the pot marigold. This hardy annual can be used as a substitute for saffron in rice or to flavor winter soups, custards, or corn bread with a tangy, peppery taste.

Chervil

Also known as French parsley, this dainty annual with light green leaves and flat clusters of white flowers is often used in French cooking, soups, sauces, and salads. It tolerates heavy frost, and its tarragon/citrus/anise-flavored leaves can be picked any time to use fresh or dried and can be frozen for future use.

Clove Pinks	The wild ancestor of the modern carnation has a spicy, mild clove flavor. The semi-double fragrant flowers of this perennial are pink to rose-purple in color and can be used fresh to flavor syrups, fruit cups, or beverages, but be sure to remove the bitter white base first.
Coriander	Flat clusters of white to pale pink flowers are followed by white, lemon-flavored seeds that resemble peppercorns. The seeds are used in curries, stir-fries, and Scandinavian breads. The leaves are referred to as cilantro and can be used in salads, soups, or salsa.
Daisy	A perennial flower with a mild flavor, the daisy can be eaten fresh in salads or be used as a garnish. Blooming from April to September, the flower has white or pink petals surrounding a yellow center. Plant six inches apart in full sun.
Dandelion	A perennial with a chicory taste when young and tender. The older leaves have a flavor similar to spinach. Dandelions can be eaten fresh, cooked, or infused, and they blend well with garlic, tarragon, chervil, and burnet. The familiar yellow flower blooms in May through July and can be minced and added to butters, spreads, and vinegar.
Day Lily	The yellow, tawny orange flowers of all day lilies are edible, but sample first to determine taste before chopping into salads or soups. Pick the flower buds after they have elongated but before they open since the smaller buds tend to taste better. When sautéed, braised, or stir-fried, they taste like a cross between asparagus and zucchini.
Dill	An annual with finely divided green foliage and clusters of edible airy, delicate yellow flowers that bloom from June to the first frost. Dill leaves flavor fish, salad dressings, and vegetables. Dillseeds, generally used as a pickling spice, are harvested by hanging flower stems upside down after seeds turn brown.
Fennel	A mild licorice flavor and an appearance similar to the dill plant characterize this perennial. Its leaves and large yellow ublema flowers should be used fresh, not dried, in soups and salads. The seeds are used in beverages, baked goods, and sausages, and the stalks can be burned to flavor grilled fish.
Scented Geraniums	A perennial generally grown as an annual or houseplant. These plants come in a wide variety of colors and scents (lemon, nutmeg, ginger, rose, peppermint), which are released by being rubbed or by the heat from the sun. Used for baked goods, ice creams, jellies, candied garnishes, and scented sugar.
Hollyhocks	The flowers are best used as an attractive container for a dish or as a garnish, but they can also be made into fritters or flavoring for tea. They have spikes of single or double flowers of every color except true blue, have a very mild taste, and are generally raised as a biennial.

Honeysuckle	Known for its delightful fragrance and sweet honey taste, this fairly invasive-growing perennial is one with which many are familiar. It can be used in puddings, ice creams, or syrups. The flowers are creamy white, yellow, pink, or red in color and bloom May to July.
Johnny-jump-ups	Blooming with brilliant violet, white, purple, or yellow flowers—or a combination of all four—it is thought to be a parent of the pansy. Its flowers make a pretty candied garnish on a dessert or can brighten up a spring salad or punch bowl. Its mild taste is reminiscent of sweet baby lettuce.
Lavender	A perennial shrub with graceful purple flowers and a perfumelike scent that is more associated with potpourri than cooking. However, its leaves and flowers can be used in vinegar or jellies, and used sparingly in salads, ice creams, and custards. English lavender is the hardiest of the species.
Lemon	The fruit of this subtropical tree, well known to us in many dishes or as a garnish, can also be jellied. Its slightly bitter, citrus taste can complement a wide range of foods. The lemon tree's white blossom has a sweet, floral fragrance that permeates the orchard.
Lemon Balm	A perennial herb with a lemony flavor and a mint undertone that prefers moist conditions. The leaves can be used generously in cooking, whole or chopped, in salads, sauces, and with poultry marinades. Its oil is used in furniture polish, and leaves can be rubbed on wooden surfaces for a similar result.
Lilac	The pyramidal lavender clusters of its flowers are known for their scent, which carries over into their taste, and can be candied or used in fritters, herb butters, scented sugars, or as a garnish. They blossom in late spring and should be picked as soon as they open.
Marigold	Although all are edible, the Tangerine Gem and Lemon Gem varieties have a more pleasant flavor, and there is a Peruvian variety often used in salsa. Most marigolds are a good accompaniment to salads, soups, and sauces and can be used as a substitute for saffron due to their taste and bright yellow coloring.
Marjoram	An aromatic herb of the mint family, marjoram has oval, velvety leaves that are good in soups, sauces, and stuffings. The tiny pinkish-white flowers, also edible, bloom in mid-summer and can be removed to increase leaf harvest. Sweet marjoram, the variety most often used in cooking, tastes like a milder, sweeter oregano.
Mint	Peppermint, spearmint, and pineapple mint are some of the varieties of this perennial. Peppermint should be used sparingly in teas or cold drinks, while spearmint can enhance lamb, jellies, salads, and chocolate. Pineapple mint provides an attractive garnish and adds zest to fruit salads or creamed cheeses.

Nasturtium

The slightly peppery taste of the young leaves, flowers, and buds combined with the vibrant oranges, reds, or yellows of this annual brighten any green salad. The flowers also provide a unique container for cold salads, but the bitter-tasting base should be removed first.

Orange

This perennial subtropical tree can reach up to 40 feet in height, and the strong sweet fragrance of its white blossoms hints at its highly perfumed, citrus taste. It can accompany other fruits, salad greens, or duck.

Oregano

The darling of Italian recipes, this pungent perennial can be used fresh or dried. It blooms June through August with white, pink, or purple flowers similar to marjoram, but it is heavier-tasting, hotter, and spicier. A wide variety of oregano is available, so look for plants with a pleasant fragrance.

Pansy

Similar in taste to Johnny-jump-ups, pansies are often used as a garnish on desserts or floating in cold drinks or soups. The flowers of this very hardy annual come in every color of the rainbow and should be picked when they first open.

Pineapple Sage

Rough, dark green leaves and bright scarlet tubular flowers that bloom in late summer characterize this tender perennial, which can be brought indoors during the winter. The flowery, pineapple taste, with a hint of sage muskiness, lends itself to seasoning fruit salads, tea, desserts, and tea breads.

Rosemary

Its dark, gray-green leaves resemble pine needles and its faint minty taste has a pine undertone. Both the leaves and spiky pale blue flowers of this tender perennial are edible. It complements lamb, poultry, beef, vegetables, and egg dishes and should be misted on hot summer days.

Roses

Older varieties seem to have more scent, therefore more taste, but many varieties can be quite bitter—so sample first. The hips (rich in vitamin C) and petals can be used for making tea, jelly, jam, syrup, or wine. The petals can also be candied or used to make rose water, scented sugar, or butter.

Sage

In ancient times its most common use was for herbal teas, but today it generally seasons poultry stuffings and sausages. It can also be found in soups, omelets, rice, breads, and vinegars, imparting a musky flavor with a hint of lemon. Harvest no more than the top third of this shrubby perennial with spikes of blue-violet flowers.

Squash Blossoms

The golden-orange flowers begin to bloom in early summer and should be picked when fully open, but don't pick them all, or there'll be no squash! The fresh squash-flavored blossoms are usually stuffed and fried, but they can also be chopped into soups, salads, or vegetable dishes. Remove stamens and pistils before cooking.

Sweet Woodruff	A staple of the May wine punch bowl, the tiny star-shaped white flowers of this shade-loving perennial can also be seen garnishing tea cakes, desserts, salads, and fruits, expecially berries. The scent of its bright green leaves, a cross between new-mown hay and vanilla, is released when they are dried.
Tarragon	The French variety is a three-foot-tall woody perennial grown from cuttings and has narrow, dark green leaves and infrequent tiny, yellow flowers. It is best when used fresh and can flavor fish, chicken, vegetables, or vinegar. Handle carefully when harvesting as they lose their oil when bruised.
Thyme	The small, gray-green leaves have a sweet, savory flavor with an earthy aroma, while the lilac-colored flowers tend to be milder with a more floral scent, perfect for garnishing salads, pastas, or desserts. This woody perennial has more than 100 species and varieties, but most work well with a wide range of dishes.
Tulip	Like the nasturtium, these brightly colored flowers are best used as a garnish or container of a cold dish, such as chicken or egg salad. They bloom in mid to late spring and their light flavor is similar in taste to peas. The best variety for culinary use is the Darwin hybrid, which has a large, single flower.
Verbena	The lance-shaped leaves of this open-growing shrub are the only lemon-scented foliage to retain its full scent after drying. It can be grown as a tender perennial or annual, and stored inside in wintertime. Its fresh or dried leaves can flavor tea, fish, poultry, vegetable marinades, salad dressings, jams, and puddings.
Violet	Like the Johnny-jump-up and pansy, it is a member of the viola family, but is a hardy perennial and has a sweeter, stronger scent. Its purple and purple-veined white flowers and heart-shaped leaves can be used as a garnish. The flowers can be made into violet water to flavor tea, breads, fruit compotes, and chilled soups.

METRIC EQUIVALENTS

Although the United States has opted to postpone converting to metric measurements, most other countries, including England and Canada, use the metric system. The following chart provides convenient approximate equivalents for allowing use of regular kitchen measures when cooking from foreign recipes.

VOLUME

These metric measures are approximate benchmarks for purposes of home food preparation.
1 milliliter = 1 cubic centimeter = 1 gram

LIQUID	DRY
1 teaspoon = 5 milliliters	1 quart = 1 liter
1 tablespoon = 15 milliliters	1 ounce = 30 grams
1 fluid ounce = 30 milliliters	1 pound = 450 grams
1 cup = 250 milliliters	2.2 pounds = 1 kilogram
1 pint = 500 milliliters	

WEIGHT

1 ounce = 28 grams
1 pound = 450 grams

LENGTH

1 inch = 2½ centimeters
¹⁄₁₆ inch = 1 millimeter

FORMULAS USING CONVERSION FACTORS

When approximate conversions are not accurate enough, use these formulas to convert measures from one system to another.

MEASUREMENTS	FORMULAS
ounces to grams:	# ounces $\times$ 28.3 = # grams
grams to ounces:	# grams $\times$ 0.035 = # ounces
pounds to grams:	# pounds $\times$ 453.6 = # grams
pounds to kilograms:	# pounds $\times$ 0.45 = # kilograms
ounces to milliliters:	# ounces $\times$ 30 = # milliliters
cups to liters:	# cups $\times$ 0.24 = # liters
inches to centimeters:	# inches $\times$ 2.54 = # centimeters
centimeters to inches:	# centimeters $\times$ 0.39 = # inches

APPROXIMATE WEIGHT TO VOLUME

Some ingredients that we commonly measure by volume are measured by weight in foreign recipes. Here are a few examples for easy reference.

flour, all-purpose, unsifted	1 pound = 450 grams = 3½ cups
flour, all-purpose, sifted	1 pound = 450 grams = 4 cups
sugar, granulated	1 pound = 450 grams = 2 cups
sugar, brown, packed	1 pound = 450 grams = 2¼ cups
sugar, confectioners'	1 pound = 450 grams = 4 cups
sugar, confectioners', sifted	1 pound = 450 grams = 4½ cups
butter	1 pound = 450 grams = 2 cups

TEMPERATURE

Remember that foreign recipes frequently express temperatures in Centigrade rather than Fahrenheit.

TEMPERATURES	FAHRENHEIT	CENTIGRADE
room temperature	68°	20°
water boils	212°	100°
baking temperature	350°	177°
baking temperature	375°	190.5°
baking temperature	400°	204.4°
baking temperature	425°	218.3°
baking temperature	450°	232°

Use the following formulas when temperature conversions are necessary.

Centigrade degrees x $\frac{9}{5}$ + 32 = Fahrenheit degrees

Fahrenheit degrees - 32 $\times$ $\frac{5}{9}$ = Centigrade degrees

AMERICAN MEASUREMENT EQUIVALENTS

1 tablespoon = 3 teaspoons	12 tablespoons = ¾ cup
2 tablespoons = 1 ounce	16 tablespoons = 1 cup
4 tablespoons = ¼ cup	1 cup = 8 ounces
5 tablespoons + 1 teaspoon = ⅓ cup	2 cups = 1 pint
8 tablespoons = ½ cup	4 cups = 1 quart
	4 quarts = 1 gallon

No-Salt Seasoning

Salt is an acquired taste and can be significantly reduced in the diet by learning to use herbs and spices instead. When using fresh herbs, use three times the amount of dried herbs. Begin with small amounts to determine your favorite tastes. A dash of fresh lemon or lime juice can also wake up your taste buds.

Herb Blends to Replace Salt

Combine all ingredients in small airtight container. Add several grains of rice to prevent caking.

No-Salt Surprise Seasoning — 2 teaspoons garlic powder and 1 teaspoon each of dried basil, oregano and dehydrated lemon juice.

Pungent Salt Substitute — 1 tablespoon dried basil, 2 teaspoons each of summer savory, celery seeds, cumin seeds, sage and marjoram, and 1 teaspoon lemon thyme; crush with pestle in mortar.

Spicy No-Salt Seasoning — 1 teaspoon each cloves, pepper and coriander, 2 teaspoons paprika and 1 tablespoon dried rosemary; crush with pestle in mortar.

Herb Complements

Beef — bay leaf, chives, cumin, garlic, hot pepper, marjoram, rosemary
Pork — coriander, cumin, garlic, ginger, hot pepper, savory, thyme
Poultry — garlic, oregano, rosemary, savory, sage
Cheese — basil, chives, curry, dill, marjoram, oregano, parsley, sage, thyme
Fish — chives, coriander, dill, garlic, tarragon, thyme
Fruit — cinnamon, coriander, cloves, ginger, mint
Bread — caraway, marjoram, oregano, poppy seeds, rosemary, thyme
Salads — basil, chives, tarragon, parsley, sorrel
Vegetables — basil, chives, dill, tarragon, marjoram, mint, parsley, pepper

Basic Herb Butter

Combine 1/2 cup (1 stick) unsalted butter, 1 to 3 tablespoons dried herbs or twice that amount of minced fresh herbs of choice, 1/2 teaspoon lemon juice and white pepper to taste. Let stand for 1 hour or longer before using.

Basic Herb Vinegar

Heat vinegar of choice in saucepan; do not boil. Pour into bottle; add 1 or more herbs of choice and seal bottle. Let stand for 2 weeks before using.

NUTRITIONAL PROFILE GUIDELINES

We have attempted to present these family recipes in a format that allows approximate nutritional values to be computed. Persons with dietary or health problems or whose diets require close monitoring should not rely solely on the nutritional information provided. They should consult their physicians or a registered dietitian for specific information.

NUTRITIONAL PROFILE ABBREVIATIONS

Cal — Calories	T Fat — Total Fat	Sod — Sodium
Prot — Protein	Chol — Cholesterol	g — grams
Carbo — Carbohydrates	Fiber — Fiber	mg — milligrams

Nutritional information is computed from information derived from many sources, including materials supplied by the United States Department of Agriculture, computer databanks and journals in which the information is assumed to be in the public domain. However, many specialty items, new products and processed foods may not be available from these sources or may vary from the average values used in these profiles. More information on new and/or specific products may be obtained by reading the nutrient labels. Unless specified, the nutritional profile of these recipes is based on all measurements being level.

- **Artificial sweeteners** vary in use and strength so should be used "to taste," using the recipe ingredients as a guideline. Sweeteners using aspartame (NutraSweet and Equal) should not be used as a sweetener in recipes involving prolonged heating, which reduces the sweet taste. For further information on the use of these sweeteners, refer to the package.
- **Alcoholic ingredients** have been analyzed for the basic ingredients, although cooking causes the evaporation of alcohol, thus decreasing caloric content.
- **Buttermilk, sour cream,** and **yogurt** are commercial types.
- **Cake mixes** that are prepared using package directions include 3 eggs and 1/2 cup of oil.
- **Chicken,** cooked for boning and chopping, has been roasted.
- **Cottage cheese** is cream-style with 4.2% creaming mixture. Dry curd cottage cheese has no creaming mixture.
- **Eggs** are all large. To avoid raw eggs that may carry salmonella, as in eggnog or 6-week muffin batter, use an equivalent amount of commercial egg substitute.
- **Flour** is unsifted all-purpose flour.
- **Garnishes,** serving suggestions, optional information, and variations are not included.
- **Margarine** and **butter** are regular, not whipped or presoftened.
- **Milk** is whole milk, 3.5% butterfat. Low-fat milk is 1% butterfat. Evaporated milk is whole milk with 60% of the water removed.
- **Oil** is any type of vegetable cooking oil. **Shortening** is hydrogenated vegetable shortening.
- **Salt** and other ingredients to taste as noted in the ingredients are not included in the profile.
- If a choice of ingredients is given, the profile reflects the first option. If a choice of amounts is given, the profile reflects the greater amount.
- Lighten-Up recipes are printed in blue, reflecting reduced values in one or more areas.

NUTRITIONAL PROFILES

Pg. No.	Recipe Title (Approx Per Serving)	Cal	Prot (g)	Carbo (g)	T Fat (g)	% Cal from Fat	Chol (mg)	Fiber (g)	Sod (mg)
10	Apricot Pickups	44	1	4	3	60	6	<1	21
10	Bleu Cheese Walnut Grapes	66	2	2	6	74	7	<1	77
11	Cherry Tomatoes w/ Herbed Cream Cheese	79	2	3	7	74	21	1	61
11	Cherry Tomatoes w/ Herbed Cream Cheese	30	3	4	<1	6	1	1	97
11	Endive Antipasto	32	1	1	3	69	4	1	134
12	Marinated Cocktail Shrimp[2]	326	15	2	28	79	135	1	570
13	Green Olive Salsa[1]	75	1	5	5	64	0	2	1046
13	Pita Crisps	11	<1	2	<1	4	0	<1	21
14	Margarita Guacamole	93	1	6	8	69	0	3	80
14	Tres Cheese Ball	136	5	2	12	80	28	<1	191
14	Tres Cheese Ball	83	6	2	6	64	14	<1	217
15	Chili Chicken Torta	203	8	3	18	79	87	<1	458
15	Chili Chicken Torta	136	9	5	9	60	34	<1	445
16	Eggplant Caviar	25	1	4	1	29	0	2	102
17	Sun-Dried Tomato and Basil Spread	221	5	4	21	82	45	1	346
17	Sun-Dried Tomato and Basil Spread	220	6	8	18	73	20	2	341
18	Artichoke-Filled Appetizer Loaf	135	5	11	7	50	18	1	290
19	Artichoke Squares	14	1	1	1	64	14	<1	46
20	Thai Chicken and Shrimp Skewers/Sauce[2]	257	22	15	13	43	51	1	1564
21	Crab Imperial Mushrooms	48	3	2	3	60	15	<1	65
22	Feta Cheese Pillows	83	2	4	7	75	23	<1	123
22	Parmesan Walnut Bruschetta	203	5	14	15	64	4	1	240
23	Michelotti's Northern Italian-Style Pizza[3]	534	17	101	6	10	0	4	585
24	Chicken and Green Chile Pinwheels	68	3	5	4	50	12	<1	126
25	Southwestern Spinach Rollers	71	1	6	5	57	6	1	126
25	Southwestern Spinach Rollers	53	2	7	2	38	2	1	133
28	Chicken and Leek Soup	223	23	23	3	13	46	2	252
29	Mushroom and Wild Rice Soup	252	12	27	11	38	1	2	1025
29	Mushroom and Wild Rice Soup	195	12	27	5	22	1	2	359
30	Vidalia Onion and Wild Mushroom Soup	152	8	13	4	22	6	2	175
31	Seafood Gazpacho	170	11	14	9	46	42	2	612
32	Garden Tomato and Zucchini Soup	76	4	8	4	39	9	2	140
33	Turkey Tortilla Soup	325	23	38	9	25	39	4	1166
33	Turkey Tortilla Soup	228	22	28	4	14	29	4	807
34	Mexicali Black Bean Chili	500	34	28	28	50	94	7	1114
34	Mexicali Black Bean Chili	392	32	29	16	37	90	7	725
35	Italian Vegetable Stew	257	8	34	11	38	0	8	465
36	Asparagus Salad with Lemon Soy Dressing	83	5	11	4	37	<1	4	133

Pg. No.	Recipe Title (Approx Per Serving)	Cal	Prot (g)	Carbo (g)	T Fat (g)	% Cal from Fat	Chol (mg)	Fiber (g)	Sod (mg)
37	Marinated Bean and Rice Salad	181	8	28	5	23	0	7	368
37	Marinated Bean and Rice Salad	156	6	24	4	24	0	5	20
38	Roasted Garlic Caesar Salad	342	11	14	27	69	26	2	488
39	Grilled Eggplant Salad[4]	502	5	11	50	87	15	4	1389
39	Grilled Eggplant Salad[7]	179	6	11	13	63	11	4	1406
39	Middle Eastern Carrot Slaw	59	2	7	2	35	9	2	37
40	Baby Greens with Red Potatoes	228	5	18	16	61	2	4	71
41	Field Greens with Rosemary Vinaigrette[5]	123	4	7	8	62	11	2	98
42	Greek Tortellini Salad	316	9	25	20	56	22	3	567
43	Shrimp and Orzo Salad	676	39	65	30	39	269	8	767
44	Wild Rice and Walnut Salad	313	7	37	16	46	0	4	441
44	Tomato, Green Bean and Basil Salad	187	2	8	17	78	0	2	11
45	Grilled Tuna Salad Niçoise	614	50	67	17	24	79	12	283
48	Grilled Beef Tenderloin with Fresh Herbs[2]	665	48	5	43	59	188	1	507
49	Flank Steak with Parmesan Rice Filling	402	35	15	21	49	103	1	620
50	Beef Tournedos with Mild Mushroom Sauté	378	38	3	21	52	129	1	272
51	Stuffed Beef Fillets with Marsala Sauce	512	45	5	31	56	128	1	560
51	Stuffed Beef Fillets with Marsala Sauce	327	38	5	14	39	109	1	196
52	Spicy Beef and Polenta	426	31	28	21	45	97	3	272
52	Spicy Beef and Polenta	363	30	28	15	36	95	3	297
53	Eggplant Parmesan and Beef Casserole	589	39	27	37	56	171	5	1619
53	Eggplant Parmesan and Beef Casserole	452	40	28	21	41	96	5	1555
54	Bourbon-Glazed Corned Beef	175	7	23	3	14	18	3	207
55	Veal Roast with Pear Salsa	169	22	5	6	30	84	1	102
56	Grilled Veal with Rum Sauce	815	60	21	47	52	268	<1	389
57	Pecan-Crusted Rack of Lamb	1615	71	26	127	71	367	3	1246
58	Roast Lamb with Potato and Tomato au Jus	411	40	22	17	37	119	3	129
59	Pork Loin w/ Red Onions and Cranberries	411	38	20	19	43	115	2	203
60	Spice Road Stuffed Pork Loin	433	48	24	16	33	134	2	117
61	Raspberry Sage Pork Chops	309	38	4	14	43	98	1	121
64	Classic Herb-Roasted Chicken	408	50	15	13	29	144	2	159
65	Calypso Chicken Breasts	361	54	13	10	25	146	1	178
66	Chicken Veronique	488	59	31	13	24	162	3	522
67	Chicken Breasts with Artichoke Hearts	483	59	36	9	16	146	4	1717
68	Un-Fried Chicken	370	57	17	7	17	147	1	649
69	Sesame-Crusted Chicken with Orange Sauce	728	65	56	27	33	176	3	793
70	Thai Peanut Chicken and Vegetables	469	32	38	22	41	63	4	1454
70	Thai Peanut Chicken and Vegetables	460	32	41	19	36	63	4	658

NUTRITIONAL PROFILES

Pg. No.	Recipe Title (Approx Per Serving)	Cal	Prot (g)	Carbo (g)	T Fat (g)	% Cal from Fat	Chol (mg)	Fiber (g)	Sod (mg)
71	Spa Cuisine Lasagna	368	35	22	15	38	97	3	954
72	Cornish Hens in Tarragon Sauce	773	58	3	56	66	361	<1	527
73	Balsamic-Glazed Salmon	333	33	9	18	49	102	<1	165
74	Salmon with Basil Vinaigrette[6,8]	741	40	50	43	52	102	8	274
75	Lime Soy Swordfish	167	24	1	7	39	45	<1	465
76	Pacific Grilled Tuna[2]	237	43	4	4	16	79	<1	573
77	Crab Manicotti	332	23	40	9	24	46	3	614
77	Crab Manicotti	287	23	40	4	12	30	4	696
78	Scallops à la Provençal	468	30	48	18	34	101	4	978
79	Roasted Red Pepper and Scallop Fettuccini	418	19	39	22	46	63	2	471
79	Roasted Red Pepper and Scallop Fettuccini	357	21	47	10	25	37	2	485
80	Scallops Florentine	189	16	4	12	57	29	1	425
81	Fettuccini with Crab and Shrimp Florentine	392	33	21	20	46	187	3	514
81	Fettuccini with Crab and Shrimp Florentine	342	34	21	14	36	179	3	549
82	Mediterranean Shrimp Pasta	398	20	48	15	33	90	3	245
82	Broccoli Bleu Cheese Linguini	499	14	37	34	60	100	4	627
83	Fettuccini with Two-Olive Sauce	342	11	36	19	47	10	3	839
83	Brie and Tomato Pasta	467	17	49	25	46	32	5	392
84	Penne with Black Beans and Artichoke Hearts	271	12	48	3	12	0	8	753
84	Greek-Style Pasta with Mint	335	11	46	12	32	22	2	465
85	Italian Vegetable Lasagna	583	38	33	34	52	104	6	727
88	Green Beans in Basil Sauce	170	3	16	12	58	0	6	20
89	California Eggplant	345	18	31	18	46	43	9	403
89	California Eggplant	280	18	33	10	31	22	9	381
90	Microwave Vidalia Onions	298	12	12	23	68	102	2	621
91	Lemon Basil Sugar Snaps	97	5	14	3	24	0	5	235
91	New Potatoes with Prosciutto	306	10	51	8	23	16	5	777
92	Moroccan New Potatoes	108	4	18	4	30	5	2	64
93	Wild Mushroom and Asparagus Risotto	318	11	40	12	35	28	2	670
93	Wild Mushroom and Asparagus Risotto	317	14	41	10	30	18	2	523
94	Persian Rice Pilaf	469	7	60	19	36	31	4	515
95	Spaghetti Squash Carbonara	593	29	46	35	52	356	10	1129
95	Spaghetti Squash Carbonara	351	30	46	8	18	37	10	1198
96	Twice-Baked Sweet Potatoes	263	4	28	16	54	31	3	527
96	Twice-Baked Sweet Potatoes	208	4	29	9	38	21	3	527
97	Summer Tomato Basil Tart	546	13	34	40	66	49	2	797
98	Yellow Peppers with Currants and Tomatoes	314	6	57	8	21	<1	4	10
99	Vegetable Tofu Stir-Fry with Almonds	251	10	15	18	61	<1	5	699

NUTRITIONAL PROFILES

Pg. No.	Recipe Title (Approx Per Serving)	Cal	Prot (g)	Carbo (g)	T Fat (g)	% Cal from Fat	Chol (mg)	Fiber (g)	Sod (mg)
100	Confetti Vegetable Fritters	92	3	10	5	45	53	2	168
100	Confetti Vegetable Fritters	62	3	10	1	19	53	2	168
101	Vegetable and Polenta Squares	311	14	42	12	33	30	6	423
104	Cheesy Egg Casserole	454	31	14	30	59	285	<1	949
105	Huevos Rancheros Casserole	488	28	24	32	58	328	3	1007
106	Mushroom and Spinach Quiche	520	16	23	41	70	218	3	638
106	Mushroom and Spinach Quiche	377	14	23	26	61	164	3	588
107	Swiss and Crab Meat Bake	469	18	17	37	70	235	2	536
107	Swiss and Crab Meat Bake	368	18	18	25	62	192	2	525
107	Hot-From-the-Oven Tomato Pie	260	6	15	20	68	26	1	613
108	Zucchini and Sausage Pie	490	19	19	37	69	220	1	768
108	Zucchini and Sausage Pie	393	22	20	25	57	186	1	992
109	Walnut Struesel Hot Cranberry Crisp	328	3	43	18	46	25	4	162
110	Cottage Biscuits	133	6	18	4	29	33	1	377
110	Iced Pecan Biscuits	327	4	41	17	46	12	1	642
110	Iced Pecan Biscuits	330	5	42	16	43	6	1	647
111	Apricot Bread	222	4	40	6	22	35	4	228
111	Apricot Bread	203	4	36	5	22	<1	4	234
112	Sugarless Banana Bread	151	3	20	7	39	18	1	337
113	Poppy Seed Bread w/ Lemon Almond Glaze	267	3	33	14	45	31	<1	202
113	Poppy Seed Bread w/ Lemon Almond Glaze	236	3	30	11	43	27	1	193
114	Sun-Dried Tomato Bread	188	7	25	7	31	43	1	716
115	Whole Wheat Garden Muffins	222	4	30	10	40	27	2	210
116	Cheddar Muffins with Apple Butter	351	9	35	19	50	89	1	533
117	Feel-No-Guilt Banana Crunch Muffins	112	3	24	1	8	1	1	168
118	Crème Brûlée French Toast	630	13	79	29	41	276	2	568
118	Crème Brûlée French Toast	574	17	84	19	30	44	2	654
118	Guiltless Stuffed French Toast	267	18	23	12	40	21	2	362
119	Whole Wheat Buttermilk Waffles	346	9	31	21	54	74	2	569
120	Oven Puff with Strawberry Sauce	461	10	52	24	46	264	1	342
120	Oven Puff with Strawberry Sauce	407	11	54	17	37	244	1	306
121	Cream Cheese Popovers	137	8	15	5	33	116	<1	293
124	Apple Lasagna	337	9	47	13	35	51	1	190
124	Apple Lasagna	273	7	49	5	18	15	1	198
125	Apricot Pecan Tassies	123	2	14	7	50	23	1	85
126	Lime Cheesecake	477	8	41	33	60	178	1	336
126	Lime Cheesecake	274	8	35	11	37	110	<1	141
127	Pecan-Topped Fudge Cheesecake	515	8	39	38	65	137	2	311

NUTRITIONAL PROFILES

Pg. No.	Recipe Title (Approx Per Serving)	Cal	Prot (g)	Carbo (g)	T Fat (g)	% Cal from Fat	Chol (mg)	Fiber (g)	Sod (mg)
128	Peach Blueberry Crisp	220	3	44	5	21	12	5	111
129	Berry Trifle	422	6	50	22	46	100	3	322
129	Berry Trifle	313	6	55	7	21	8	4	489
130	Poached Pears with Raspberry Sauce	333	2	83	1	4	0	9	8
131	Italian Strawberry Ice	248	1	50	<1	2	0	3	6
132	Decadent Truffles	93	1	9	7	61	8	1	15
132	Miraculously Easy Pralines	120	1	14	8	54	11	1	14
133	Almond Joy Cake	670	7	87	36	46	64	4	363
133	Almond Joy Cake	414	5	54	22	45	39	2	229
134	Grandma's Traditional Apple Cake	585	5	65	35	53	35	2	108
135	Tropical Carrot Cake	246	5	51	3	12	5	1	347
136	Chocolate Pecan Torte Cake	794	9	70	59	63	233	4	77
137	Chocolate Intimidator	689	8	45	59	71	205	2	413
138	Brickle Crunch Cookies	141	2	14	9	55	14	1	97
139	Fudge Sundae Cookies	132	3	16	7	45	13	1	92
140	White Chocolate Biscotti	104	2	13	5	44	19	<1	78
141	Lemon Coconut Bars	209	2	29	10	43	29	1	104
142	Lemon Shortbread /Glaze	227	2	23	14	56	38	1	128

[1]Nutritional profile includes the entire amount of wine vinegar.

[2]Nutritional profile includes the entire amount of marinade.

[3]Nutritional profile is available only for the crust.

[4]Nutritional profile includes the entire amount of salt and olive oil.

[5]Nutritional profile includes the entire amount of vinaigrette.

[6]Nutritional profile includes the entire amount of Basil Vinaigrette.

[7]Nutritional profile includes the entire amount of salt.

[8]Nutritional profile does not include Asian red chili paste with garlic.

≤ 25% of calories from fat and ≤ 50 grams cholesterol.

 ≤ 200 milligrams sodium.

INDEX

Recipes & Remedies

California Pharmacists Association
1112 I Street, Suite 300
Sacramento, California 95814
pubs@cpha.com

Please send me _____ copies of *Recipes & Remedies* at $19.95 each $ _____

Postage and handling at $5.00 each $ _____

California residents add applicable sales tax $ _____

Total $ _____

_____
Name

_____
Address

_____
City   State   Zip

_____
Telephone   email address

Method of Payment: [   ] MasterCard   [   ] VISA

[   ] Check payable to California Pharmacists Association

_____
Account Number   Expiration Date

_____
Cardholder Name

_____
Signature

Photocopies will be accepted.